Using UML Activities to model Business Processes

A Handbook for Practitioners

by

Ed Walters

"as for me, all I know is that I know nothing" - Socrates

COPYRIGHT AND TRADEMARK NOTICES

CONTENTS

1. INTRODUCTION

Why write this Handbook.

A Handbook is *"... a type of reference work, or other collection of instructions, that is intended to provide ready reference"[Wikipedia]*. This Handbook is on the subject of using Activities and Activity Diagrams, as defined by the Unified Modeling Language (UML), to model Business Processes. As such it may be useful to architects, analysts and designers who are engaged in modeling enterprise processes for whatever reason.

I confess I am an admirer of short books and articles that focus on a specific topic, define a limited scope and deal with it comprehensively and authoritatively. In this regard I have a few heroes, including the original C manual from Kernighan and Ritchie [1] and Martin Fowler's UML Distilled [2]. It would be invidious of me to name any of my own personal villains, so I won't.

On the other hand, I am also an admirer of UML, which might seem contradictory, given the 800+ pages of rather dense language that the current specification manages to fill up. If I may be permitted to borrow and adapt a famous phrase of Lord Palmerston, it's possible only 3 people have ever understood the whole of the UML – one is dead, one is mad and the third has forgotten[1].

However I believe we must forgive the authors of UML for their verbosity. Specifications of this kind are not meant to be read by ordinary mortals cover to cover[2]. It is down to secondary literature, like this one, to interpret the holy script for specific domains. This is my motivation therefore for the production of this Handbook, coupled with the rather surprising discovery that there isn't a lot of comprehensive and well-informed literature already out there on this specific topic. Scott Ambler as usual makes a reasonable attempt at providing a quick summary of the notation for Activity Diagrams [6]. There are a series of articles in the Journal of Object Technology [7] by Conrad Bock, explaining Actions and Activities and their notations. Bock, however, is one of the Technical Leads on this subject for the Object Management Group (OMG), so you might find his articles rather heavy going. I hope readers will find this humble work situated somewhere in between the scope and goals of these two respected and world-renowned authors.

---

[1] The British statesman Lord Palmerston is reported to have said: "Only three people have ever really understood the Schleswig-Holstein business—the Prince Consort, who is dead—a German professor, who has gone mad—and I, who have forgotten all about it." [source: Wikipedia]
[2] So a moment of somber reflection please for those poor tool vendors who have to do this.

The importance of at least being able to read and interpret Activity Diagrams stems from the fact that UML is a de facto standard for describing systems of any kind, and is therefore universal in its application. There are many specialized languages in use for describing specific domains[3], but UML remains a widely adopted and well supported language with which to represent the architecture of any 'system-of-interest'. Although there are alternatives to UML for modeling Business Processes[4], UML Activities and their notation are an option worthy of consideration, especially in those situations where associated software developers are using UML too.

1.1 Conventions used in this Handbook.

References to 'you' are to you, the Reader, to 'I' are references to me, and to 'we' are references to you, me or anybody else.

References to the 'Spec' are blanket references to the UML specification document [UML]. References to other supporting resources and publications are numbered in square brackets – e.g. [1].

Specific references to parts of the Spec are labelled [UML: *ref*], where ref is a numbered section of the Spec or a reference to a figure copied from the Spec.

When discussing aspects of business modeling, certain words or phrases have a reserved meaning. Such words or phrases have their first letter(s) capitalized. Thus for example 'Business Process' refers to a specific type of process.

The Spec itself tends to use 'upper camel case' to label the concepts defined in the UML metamodel[5] – for example ExecutableNode. So if I am referring to a concept defined in the Spec, I will follow this convention, and use a different font to emphasize that it is a concept that has significance in terms of the UML language. The exceptions are for the words 'Activity' and 'Action' and their plurals, which occur often, and don't need any more emphasis, in my opinion.

Similarly any properties of the metamodel concepts defined in UML are written in 'lower camel case'. I use italics to emphasize the use of a UML-

---

[3] Such as ArchiMate for representing Enterprise Architecture.
[4] A list that would include IDEF, BPMN and ARIS.
[5] The metamodel in this context is a model of some aspect of the modelling language itself. The Spec is liberally sprinkled with metamodels, defining the structure of the UML language, including Activities and Actions.

defined metamodel property – for example *isSingleInstance* is a property of an Activity.

Some diagrams in the Handbook are incomplete, and may only contain what is necessary to demonstrate some aspect of UML Activities. I generally refer to these as 'fragments'.

1.2 Self-Publishing

Finally I would ask you to bear in mind the self-publishing nature of this work, and forgive my all too obvious incompetence with the formatting of Word documents, which sometimes move in mysterious ways, their wonders to perform. I would be most grateful to receive any feedback or comments on the Handbook, on its contents, format or structure: truecom@ntlworld.com

2. NOTES ON MODELING IN GENERAL

On the nature of models and modeling.

Modeling is an inevitable part of the process by which human beings solve problems. As an activity, it always sits on the pathway between a problem and its solution, although the problem solver may have some freedom to choose the degree of formality and ceremony with which this activity is undertaken.

UML defines what it means by a model:

"A model is always a model of something. The thing being modeled can generically be considered a system within some domain of discourse. The model then makes some statements of interest about that system, abstracting from all the details of the system that could possibly be described, from a certain point of view and for a certain purpose." [UML: §16.3.1]

A model is therefore an abstract description of some 'system-of-interest', as-is or to-be, and may serve a number of purposes as part of problem solving, including:

-Serving as a communication tool, and as a basis for discussing some important features of a system-of-interest.
-Revealing to the modeler what they know and what they don't know, prompting their search for further information.
-Providing documentation, and a way of recording knowledge, especially if the model and its elements are stored in an electronic repository.

A good model is one that is useful in any of the contexts above. A model should be accurate in what it does show, but will omit many features of the system-of-interest that are not relevant for the purpose that the modeler has in mind.[6]

In systems analysis and design, at least, there is a strong tradition and preference, stretching back over many years, for visual modeling and for the use of diagrams. Nonetheless it is also recognized that there are definite limits on what we can expect to model visually – if we are not careful the complexity of the graphics themselves can become self-defeating! Hence the visual aspect of any model will generally need complementing with

---

[6] These thoughts are at the centre of George Box's famous aphorism "Essentially all models are wrong, but some are useful" [11]. All models are incomplete approximations of reality, as Box makes clear, but we can't expect to solve problems without using them.

textual documentation of some kind.

A familiar example of a model is a map. Let's take the London 'tube' map as an example.

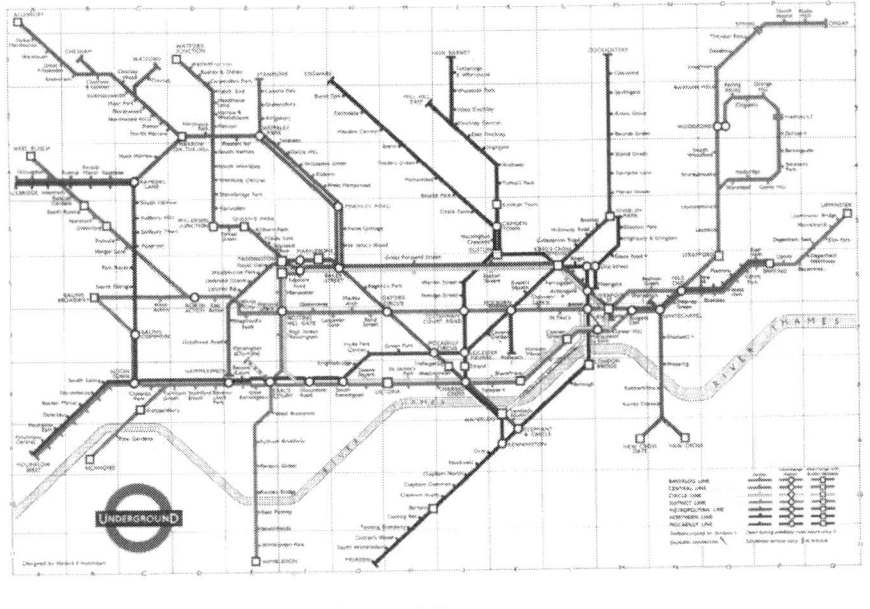

Figure 1: Map of the London Underground System

The diagram in Fig. 1 is part of a model of the London Underground railway system (the 'Tube') which would be useful for a traveler who wishes to get from A to B. Supporting the visual aspect of this diagram we would expect there to be a timetable of train services, station access information and other material. The *model* is therefore the *map* plus all the supporting *texts*.

This model is fine for travelers, but we would not expect such a model to be much use to engineers needing to maintain the railway's signaling system, for example. Hence we may conclude that each model of a system is only useful to a defined audience for a defined purpose, and therefore the modeler must be clear about such parameters from the outset, in order to build a successful model.

Furthermore, the development of a model is bound to be an iterative and evolutionary task, as indeed was the case of the Tube map[7]. Models are drafted and re-drafted many times, until there is agreement that they are

---

[7] Cf: https://londonist.com/2016/05/the-history-of-the-tube-map

good enough. If they are preserved, they will also need adapting as time moves on.

Naturally all of this is true of the modeling of Business Processes. There is not just one interesting aspect of a Business Process, but potentially many, which brings us to the important idea of Views.

2.1 Views

Given that there is some system-of-interest whose specification we wish to work on, such as a Business Process, there may be many stakeholders, with many different interests in it. It is the job of the modeler to expose the relevant features of the system to each of the stakeholders via the use of appropriate *Views*.[8] A View should be a complete description of the system, from the perspective of a particular stakeholder's concern, and it should be pitched at a suitable level of abstraction for the stakeholder's needs. A View is delivered by building one or more models of the system.

Thus we have to get used to the idea that isn't possible to produce a single View of a Business Process that would satisfy all possible stakeholders. The modeler therefore needs to be clear about the audience for their process model, and perhaps has to consider different models for different audiences. For example UML Activity Diagrams can focus on the *flow of control* of the process or the *data flow* in the process. Although any Activity Diagram could show both types of flow, would there be an audience for this? And there may be many other valid Views of a Business Process, ones focused on governance, on regulation, on security etc.

Given that any model is only ever an approximation of the real thing, the modeler must also address the question of how precise the model has to be for the audience in question. In my experience, any model, UML or otherwise, that is used to support discussions with the business community directly, would need to be a fairly informal model, whilst the model used for discussions with a more technical audience would need to be more precise.

A common enough modelling problem therefore is how to maintain all these different Views synchronized, since they all refer in the end to the specification of a single system. This brings us to the need to maintain a single central Repository.

2.2 Need for a Repository; "One Version of the Truth"

---

[8] The definitive guide to Views in the context of the architecture of a system-of-interest is usually taken to be ISO 42010 [4]. This document distinguishes View from *Viewpoint*, which is the term used for the *definition* of a View.

Given the potential variety of Views and audiences, the question naturally arises as to how to maintain consistency and coherence between the features shown in distinct Views. For every system-of-interest that we are working on, we would ideally store all the knowledge about that system in a single place, and use Views to expose selected features of it. Views may contain features of the target system that could be cross-referenced with features included in other Views, so there is a general need for any of the elements of the system's description to be visible from any View.

There is also the need to maintain links between distinct Views of similar aspects of the system which are pitched at differing levels of abstraction. For example a link between Analysis and Design artifacts.

We will see in the next chapter how UML deals with this, but the solution in principal is to maintain the entire body of knowledge concerning all the features of the system-of-interest in a single Repository. Views can then be seen as selective expositions, via models, of the same underlying Repository for a purpose and for an audience.

Whilst all this may sound like common sense, it is not so easy to do in practice, especially in an enterprise context. The pressure to solve problems quickly is intense, and there is inevitably some overhead in maintaining any form of centralized Repository. Tools can certainly help to ease the maintenance burden, but many enterprises, including some famous names I am personally familiar with, are ill-equipped in this regard, and fail to appreciate the need for adequate governance of this corporate imperative.

2.3 Need for a Style Guide

As a final note on modeling in general, it is usually important to develop a *Style Guide* for use by a modeling team, to ensure consistency in the use of the modeling language. Like natural language, a modeling language like UML can express the same thing in many different ways, hence the need for stylistic guidelines. I will make the odd comment about stylistic considerations in the text ahead.

3. INTRODUCING UML

What is UML and why use it to model Business Processes. UML's view of the architecture of any system. Extending UML.

UML stands for the 'Unified Modeling Language' [UML]. This is a standard owned and administered by the Object Management Group, OMG [3]. Many books recount the story of how UML came to be, so I will not revisit that history here. If you would like to read up more information on this, [8] is my recommendation.

UML is described by the OMG website as:

"A specification defining a graphical language for visualizing, specifying, constructing, and documenting the artifacts of distributed object systems." [https://www.omg.org/Spec/UML].

The specification current at the time of writing, and therefore the one I have used here, is at version 2.5.1, December 2017. In this specification the purpose of UML is stated:

"The objective of UML is to provide system architects, software engineers, and software developers with tools for analysis, design, and implementation of software-based systems as well as for modeling business and similar processes." [UML: §1]

3.1 Object Orientation 101

The principle focus and *raison d'être* of UML is therefore related to software engineering, hence 'system' in this context is by default a software system, and in fact an Object Orientated (OO) software system. OO software systems are recognized as best practice these days, because they are flexible, modular and easy to adapt. OO is supported by a number of modern programming languages.

Software that is OO relies on a collaboration of software objects to deliver the required functionality of the system. The characteristics of objects are defined by classes; thus it is said by OO folks that an object as an *instance* of a class.

Thinking about the world in terms of objects is a fairly natural process for human beings. Classifying objects is a fairly natural process too, human beings seem to be good at this.

For example the general characteristics of all Customers could be modeled as a Class called 'Customer', and a real Customer, say 'Smith', could then be thought of as an object belonging to that class, an instance of that class. Customer 'Brown' would be another, distinct, instance.

A UML Class may have *attributes* and *operations* defined for it. An attribute, aka *property*, of the Customer class could be, for example, *customerName*, which holds the name of the Customer. Both the Smith object and the Brown object will have this attribute, because they are objects of the Customer class. The value of the attribute *customerName* for the Smith object is 'Smith', and for the Brown object it is 'Brown'.

Operations define the behavior that we could ask an object to perform for us. Each object gets a copy of the operations defined for their class. So for example we could define an operation for the Customer class, let's say *getName()*, which looks up and returns the value of *customerName* for a specific object. If we invoked this operation on the Smith object, we would get the value 'Smith' back as a result. OO software works by objects invoking each other's behavior, passing data and information around in the process.

Fortunately you don't have to be a software developer, or an expert on OO, to be able to use UML Activities and Activity Diagrams for modeling Business Processes successfully. OO thinking does have some relevance though. For example, it is important to recognize the distinction between a process or a task as a Class, which has a specification that you the modeler build, and the instances of that process or task which actually run in BaU[9].

It's also important to consider in our enterprise models what structures support, or should support, required behaviors. Looking at this through an OO lens is helpful here. Hopefully this Handbook will throw light upon such matters as we go along.

3.2 Why use UML for modeling Business Processes

A reasonable question to ask at this point is why use a software specification language to model enterprise processes.

The answer to this lies in the fundamental nature of all systems. If one is prepared to see *any* system-of-interest as a collection of collaborating parts that pursues some goal or other, then UML can be successfully used in domains quite different to software engineering, including people activity systems like enterprises. The secret of UML's continuing success, in this regard, is that UML has built-in extension mechanisms that make it a very

---

[9] **Business as U**sual; i.e. normal routine business operations.

flexible modeling instrument. I will discuss these mechanisms briefly later in this chapter.

That said, it is inevitable that there are some features of UML which are obviously software-centric, and I will make the odd comment on this, whenever we come across them.

3.3 Modeling with UML

The central purpose of UML therefore is to facilitate the creation, via modeling, of a specification for a system in sufficient detail to guide the construction and deployment of the real thing, which, in the case of software, takes the form of deployed binary code, offered as a service to end-users. Let us take a look in this section at how UML understands the modeling process itself, as part of problem solving.

The authors of UML appreciate that modelers will usually want to adopt a stepwise approach to doing the modeling work, and therefore there are, at least, three different specification levels at which UML is expected to be used by analysts and designers who are working on a system:

-As a sketch of the required system. Informal use of UML to facilitate discussions around the essence of the software needed to solve a problem.

-As a blueprint. A stricter form of specification and one which the eventual software should more or less be consistent with.

-As a programming language. A specification with enough detail to be turned into a machine readable form, executable by a computer, either directly, or via mapping to a suitable popular coding language, like Java, C# etc.

So modelers could start with a visual sketch of the software system, then refine that model into a blueprint, and finally embellish the blueprint with enough detail to generate most of the code. This is the basis of a longstanding OMG initiative called *Model Driven Architecture*, or MDA.

UML is widely used in software engineering circles for doing sketches, alongside other sketching and text-based techniques. Simply using the UML visual notation is sufficient for these purposes, so diagrams can be hand-drawn or made using a lightweight drawing tool, like Visio. Such sketches might be thrown away after use.

To create the blueprint of a software system it is necessary to make use of some kind of Repository, the sort I referred to in the previous chapter. In

UML the basic unit of organization of specification features is the *Package*, which you could think of as a folder, whilst a View in UML is called a *Model*, which is a specialization of the Package concept. Modeling software, or anything else in UML, means creating at least one Model (which I will henceforth refer to as 'the Model'), and possibly several depending on the need. Each Model may contain a number of specification items, including diagrams and textual documents. Each element of the system the modeler has defined, either directly or via UML diagrams, will be found in the Model, and any non-visual aspects of these elements would be maintainable there.

Some thought is required as to the organization of Models when we embark upon a modeling task, whether that be for software or Business Processes or anything else. However a detailed discussion of the options here is beyond the scope of this Handbook, and in any case, you will need to study the capabilities offered to you by the tool you are using. Just remember in reading the text ahead that references to the 'Model' are references to the system's complete specification, both visual and non-visual, from a particular point of view. In our particular use case, the point of view is Business Process modeling, which is a View of an enterprise system.

To reach the level at which a UML specification could be turned into a machine readable form, the modeler would need to create considerable additional detail using a tool's Model facilities directly, documenting details of the elements that don't have a visual notational form. This level of use of UML is generally dubbed the *implementer* level, and is very uncommon, which isn't surprising, given that even blueprint activity is relatively rare.

It is possible to export a UML Model as an XML-style message, whose format is standardized, which yields a machine readable storage format that software could exploit for some purpose. For example an Activity could be converted into a BPEL[10] script, if the Model information was rich enough.

My fervent wish is that this Handbook will be of use to both sketchers and blueprinters, inclining perhaps more towards the latter. Implementers I'm afraid will have to look elsewhere for advice. A good book on that subject would make interesting reading.

3.4 Concerning the fundamental Architecture of Systems

In order to fully appreciate the nature of UML Activities it is useful to recognize how UML understands the fundamental architecture of any given

---

[10] Business Process Execution Language. So in theory, a UML Activity could be turned into a script that supports a workflow process.

system-of-interest.

According to UML, the specification of the architecture of a system consists of a mixture of structural and behavioral elements, which have relationships with one another.[11] Although we generally consider that the value offered by a system to its Customers or Users is derived from its behavior, behaviors require structures to execute them, and behaviors must act upon structures to produce the required value.

This approach to 'the architecture of anything' can be illustrated by thinking about a person opening and closing a door.

Figure 2: A Door

Let us imagine modeling a person going into and out of a room several times a day, using a door like the one in Fig. 2. What are the behaviors and structures in the architecture of this 'system'?

Behaviors in this example include entering and leaving the room. Structures include the door, the room and the person entering or leaving the room. The value offered by this system is the ability to enter or leave the room, but the dependency of behavior upon appropriate structures is clear enough from this example; i.e. there can be no behavior without structures.

---

[11] This is mainstream thinking in Enterprise Architecture too.

With respect to structures, it is useful to distinguish between 'active structures' and 'passive structures'[12]. Active structures perform or exhibit behavior – in this example the active structure is the 'person'. Passive structures have behavior performed upon them in some way, in this example the 'door' and the 'room'.

The defining characteristic of behavior is that of a temporal sequence of actions, triggered by an event. Behavior is what an active structure *does* when prompted by an event. In our example 'open the door' and 'enter the room' are therefore behaviors. We can imagine the prompting event is the desire of the person to enter the room, or to leave it.

For the purpose, at least, of modeling Business Processes, we can distinguish two types of behavior[13]:

-What we might call 'read-only' behavior. This is behavior that doesn't change the state of the system in any significant way. UML refers to this as behavior with 'no side effects'. For example a person approaching a door could perform the behavior of checking to see if the door was open or closed. This behavior doesn't change the state of the door.

-What we might call 'change' behavior which does change the state of the system's structures in a significant way. So making a closed door open, or vice versa, would be a change behavior.

Change behaviors are the ones that are most important to those of us concerned with the analysis and design of Business Processes, because it is only through changes to certain structures, or their configuration, that enterprises can create value. The effect of a behavior on structures may be transient, only lasting while the behavior lasts, or it may be permanent.

Returning to our door illustration, it is important to appreciate that a new behavior instance is created every time the triggering event occurs. So the behavior 'enter the room', for example, may occur many times a day. Each new behavior, though, must rely on existing structures, which in this case are the person and the door. There is not a new door every time the person enters the room, nor indeed a new person.

One implication of all this is that, for behavior to occur in a real system-of-

---

[12] This distinction is not from UML. I got this idea from ArchiMate, but the ArchiMate authors may have got it from elsewhere.

[13] UML doesn't explicitly use this terminology. And nor would a physicist, I suspect; any behavior must affect a system, even if the effect is just a use of energy. Nonetheless, I find this crude distinction convenient for the purposes of understanding behavior in UML Activities.

interest, the system must possess some relatively permanent active structures, which can recognize events. Enterprises do possess such things, in the shape of people, and increasingly, IT systems.

3.5 UML Diagram Types

In view of the previous sections, you will not be surprised to discover that UML splits its diagram types between structure types and behavior types. The purpose of this Handbook is to explain the use of Activities, and its visual notation as Activity Diagrams, which is a behavior diagram type. Since Business Processes are a very important form of enterprise behavior, performed by enterprises on enterprise structures, Activities are an obvious way to model them in UML.

The 'hard yards' of the specification work for defining a Business Process will be possible by using a UML-compliant tool to create an Activity Diagram within a Model. But not all of the features of Activities have a visual notation, so the specification of an Activity is not its diagram. Even those Activity elements that do have a visual notation, could have specification properties that don't appear on the diagram. Such properties are all defined in the UML standard, and the Handbook will point these out wherever I think they have business modeling significance.

It's also worth commenting that there are probably quite a few important aspects of Business Process modeling that aren't covered explicitly by Activities. An example of this is a commonly used Task property like 'Measure of Performance'. Nonetheless it is relatively simple to add these features into a Business Process specification, by using UML's extension mechanisms, which I will review next.

3.6 Extending UML

UML has built-in features that allow it to be extended. This means that the basic UML language can be adapted for specific domains quite distinct from software systems. An example of this is adapting UML so that it can be used to describe a physical database schema. Another example is the outstanding and seminal work done by Eriksson and Penker in adapting UML for modeling Business Architecture [9].

The basic extension mechanism is called *profiling*. If we wanted to extend UML for use in a specific domain, we would create a Profile and apply that to our Model.

The most significant part of a Profile uses a mechanism called *stereotyping* to derive a new semantic element from an existing one, extending the ones offered by UML natively. A stereotype is indicate visually by using guillemets, which are the quotation mark symbols used in the French language (« »).

For example we could create a Profile called 'Business Process Modeling' and within it stereotype a native UML concept like 'Activity' as «Business Process». It could even have its own icon. Once we point our new Profile to our system's Model, the stereotype becomes available to us in our diagrams and Activity specifications.

Additional properties, known as *Tagged Values*, can be defined for a stereotype. Tagged Values provide a mechanism for creating metadata about the new concept, extending any provided by UML natively. A stereotype can also be defined with attributes, which is particularly interesting in this context, since we will inevitably have the need to document certain attributes of Business Processes, Tasks and other elements like Actors etc. So, for example, an attribute that could be added to a «Business Process» is *'processOwner'*. The value of such attributes could then be maintained by the enterprise function that manages the enterprise's processes.[14]

A stereotype can also be defined with *Constraints*, which capture any rules that must be observed when including an existing or new type in a Model. An example of a constraint for a «Business Process» could include standard preconditions and postconditions, which I will discuss later. Constraints can be expressed in any form of language, but you should be aware that OMG owns and administers a standard called Object Constraint Language (OCL) that is often used for this purpose.

Finally, in the Spec itself, there is something called the Standard Profile, in which a number of standard extensions have already been registered. All conforming tools should support these extensions, so they are available in any Model, without the need to apply the Profile explicitly. We will see a few examples of the use of these standard stereotypes in the narrative that follows.

---

[14] There are a number of UML Profiles on offer out there in cyberspace for modeling Business Processes, some of which you will have to pay for. This is a topic still undergoing development, so we are well short of a recognized standard at this time. Indeed there is not even a widely acknowledged metamodel for Business Process Modeling yet, and obviously one would be needed to create a standard Profile.

4. MODELING BUSINESS PROCESSES

A discussion about the nature of Business Processes, and how to go about modeling them. Also comments concerning the suitability of UML Activities as a means of doing so.

Every modeler has to have a clear understanding of the nature of the system-of-interest they are modeling. Experience has taught me that it can't be taken for granted that everyone will have the same understanding of what a Business Process is, along with its attributes and characteristics, so what follows is a summary of my understanding of this topic. This understanding underpins the modeling approach using UML, shown in later chapters.

The English word *process* simply signifies a specification of how a result of some kind is meant to be achieved:

"a series of actions or steps taken in order to achieve a particular end" *[Source: OED]*.

A widely accepted definition of a Business Process goes something like this:

"a group of Tasks that together create a result of value to a Customer"[10]

In an enterprise context, a well-formed Business Process manipulates the enterprise's resources to achieve a desirable output, and by doing so creates value for some stakeholder(s). I think the following are all significant features of a Business Process, seen from the perspective of Business Architecture:

- Business Processes define the detailed behavior of the enterprise. When an agent like the enterprise changes something, changes its inputs into its outputs for example, we can refer to that 'doing activity' as enterprise behavior. It is an enterprise's ability to perform behaviors that justifies its existence, for that is the only way that value can be created.
- One view of an enterprise is therefore as a collection of the behaviors we call Business Processes.
- Business Processes *orchestrate* the resources of an enterprise; resources such as time, people, information, raw materials, IP, installations etc. Resources are acquired and deployed by an enterprise because behaviors need them. Some resources have intrinsic value, others little or none, but orchestration is always needed to leverage real enterprise value from these resources.

-Most Business Processes exhibit a *workflow* format[15]. Workflow implies a temporal sequence of steps, or Tasks, triggered by a Business Event. The phrase 'end-to-end' is often used in this context, meaning that we try to document all the consequences of the triggering event, which are traced out by the workflow definition.

-The model of a Business Process should identify a well-defined beginning (start point) and a well-defined end (end point)[16]. It is the need to arrive at such clear definitions that is one of the justifications for engaging in the modeling effort.

-All the work of an enterprise should be contained within at least one Business Process. Otherwise why is it being done? What value does it create?

-Business Processes cost money to execute. Thus two very important aspects of an enterprise system, which is how does it create value and what does it spend money on, are captured in the analysis and design of its Business Processes.

4.1 Complexity and Granularity

But there is a problem which we encounter pretty quickly as we approach the modeling of Business Processes, and that is how do we identify where and when a process is needed? Enterprises exhibit complex behavior patterns. If we attempt to model an enterprise's behavior at the lowest level of granularity directly, we will be overwhelmed by the complexity of the result. This would counteract the benefits we expected to get from the modeling effort.

In fact the enemy here *is* complexity; we must have an effective strategy for dealing with complexity or it will surely defeat us. The approach that is usually taken for dealing with such complexity, is to define different levels of granularity of behavior modeling, integrated into a hierarchy. Something like the modeling approach shown in Fig. 3 is generally deemed necessary.

---

[15] Not all processes have this characteristic, as we shall see later.
[16] Conceivably several beginning and/or ends, but all well-defined.

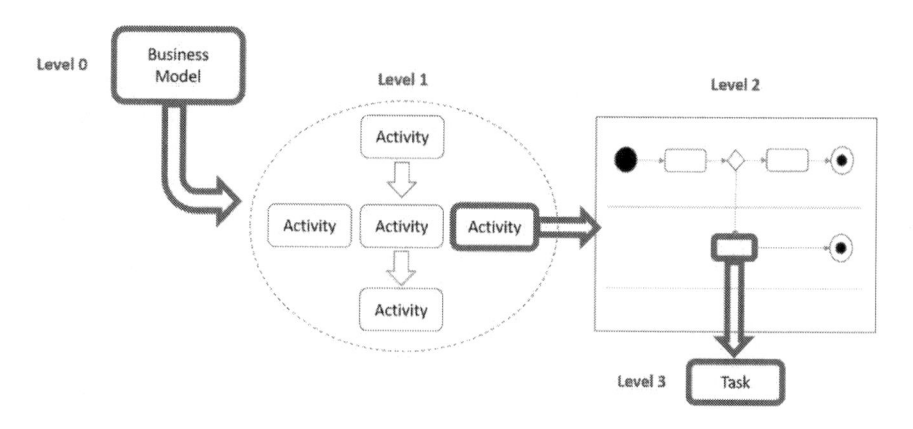

Figure 3: Organizing behavior modeling for an enterprise

The description of these levels is as follows:

- *Level 0:* This level views the enterprise as a black box. We can see the Value Proposition[17] of the enterprise, and some of the key parameters that define the enterprise's Business Model. Some core behaviors might be identified.[18]

- *Level 1:* Commonly known as the Activity or Capability level, we can see what the enterprise needs to be able to do in order to deliver on its Value Proposition. This is a coarse-grained view of behaviors. At this level behaviors have dependencies, but not sequences. At this level we may also define Value Streams, which are the linking together of Capabilities to create value for stakeholders.

- *Level 2:* This is the level most commonly associated with the term 'process model'. Level 2 modeling will usually consist of some form of 'flow chart', so this is where the UML Activity Diagram will come in handy. It's worth noting that in practice Level 2 may need to contain a few sub-levels, always seeking to control the complexity of the model effectively.

- *Level 3:* The atomic level of enterprise behavior modeling, associated with a single atomic business transaction. It is common to label this as a Task. The scope of a Task may be described by the acronym OPOPOT – a piece of work carried out by **O**ne **P**erson, in **O**ne **P**lace, at **O**ne **T**ime. This is a useful guideline, especially if we are expecting to proceed to the specification of a software application in support of the process.

---

[17] The Value Proposition is a key part of the expression of the fundamental purpose of the enterprise. What value does the enterprise offer to its Customers?

[18] See for example the Business Model Canvas format for representing a Business Model. [5].

The modeling of this hierarchy can be approached from both a top-down and a bottom-up perspective, and generally we would expect to do both. Top-down modeling answers the question of what behavior *should* be there, in line with the Value Proposition and the enterprise's current strategy. Bottom-up modeling attempts to organize what behavior *actually* does go on. Comparing these views of behavior will help Management to understand where to direct their investments in business change and improvement initiatives, including the use of IT.

4.2 Suitability of UML Activities for modeling Enterprise Behavior

It is possible to model this entire hierarchy of enterprise behaviors using UML Activities. This Handbook focuses principally on modeling at Level 2, but there are a few notes further on about UML modeling at other levels, although I must admit this is not a common practice by any means.

In support of my claim that Activities are a suitable way to model enterprise behaviors, let us examine what UML says about behavior.

"Behavior is the basic concept for modeling dynamic change. Behavior may be executed, either by direct invocation or through the creation of an active object that hosts the behavior. Behavior may also be emergent, resulting from the interaction of one or more participant objects that are themselves carrying out their own individual behaviors." [UML: §13.1]

The notion of a behavior is tied to the notion of an event. In a sense, event and behavior are two sides of the same coin. An event is created by some noteworthy occurrence, like a change of state or a point in time, which is recognized as significant by the system-of-interest. A significant event provokes behavior in the system-of-interest as a planned way of reacting to it.

Another explanation of behavior in the Spec makes the role of events clear:

"A Behavior is a specification of events that may occur dynamically over time (see also sub clause 13.3 on the explicit modeling of Events in UML). This specification may be prescriptive of specifically what events may occur in what situations, descriptive of emergent behavior or illustrative of possible sequences of event occurrences. Every Behavior defines at least one event, the event of its invocation." [UML: §13.2.3.1]

These explanations of behavior align closely with my earlier notes concerning the nature of Business Processes. A Business Process is triggered by a Business Event and its Tasks produce changes in the enterprise's resources as the process instance progresses over time. Business

Processes also produce events and respond to events during their execution; in fact, it is possible to model a Business Process as a sequence of events[19].

It would seem then that UML Activities are a suitable modelling device for the representation of Business Processes, in certain Views. As we shall see, we expect to be able to model a Business Process as a UML Activity, and it's Tasks as Actions. There are at least two main purposes for this type of model, which may serve distinct audiences:

-To show a temporal sequence of Tasks that make up the Business Process, i.e. the workflow.
-To show the manipulation of data and other passive resources by Tasks throughout the Business Process.

I will start the exploration of the topic by concentrating in the next few chapters on using Activities to model the first purpose listed above, which is by far the most common usage. Later in the Handbook I will take a look at the second usage.

Finally, and harking back to my earlier comments concerning Profiles, I should say that the purpose of the Handbook is to explain the semantics of Activities, and shows them applied to the domain of Business Process modeling. You though, as the enterprise modeler, may need to approach the modeling task from another angle, by first defining a metamodel for the modeling of Business Processes that you and your team are content with, and then use the information in the Handbook to express this in UML.

---

[19] Which is the approach taken by modeling languages like ARIS. This modeling style is called an EPC – Event Process Chain.

5. ELEMENTARY FLOW CONTROL NOTATION

Introducing Activities and the Activity Diagram with some of its basic elements and notations.

An *element* is a *'constituent of a model'* *[UML: §7.8.6.1]*. Elements are what we can use to build a model. Think of them as building blocks, like a range of differently shaped Lego bricks. Most UML elements have a notation to represent them visually in a diagram, although they may have properties that don't show up visually.

An Activity can be described using the elements defined for Actions and Activities in UML. These are two separate parts of the Spec, because Actions can be used in all three UML behavior model types; Activities, State Machines and Interactions.

This is how UML describes an Action:

"An Action is the fundamental unit of behavior specification in UML. An Action may take a set of inputs and produce a set of outputs, though either or both of these sets may be empty. Some Actions may modify the state of the system in which the Action executes. Actions are contained in Behaviors, specifically Activities (as ExecutableNodes, see Clause 15) and Interactions (see Clause 17)." UML: §16.1].

This is how UML describes an Activity :

"An Activity is a kind of Behavior (see sub clause 13.2) that is specified as a graph of nodes interconnected by edges. A subset of the nodes are executable nodes that embody lower-level steps in the overall Activity. Object nodes hold data that is input to and output from executable nodes, and moves across object flow edges. Control nodes specify sequencing of executable nodes via control flow edges. Activities are essentially what are commonly called "control and data flow" models".[20] [UML: §15.1].

The only executable node is the Action, so an Activity is a collection of Actions, showing how the Actions are coordinated for some purpose.

5.1 Graph of Nodes

A useful metaphor for the way an Activity works is to think of it as a circuit board, like the one in Fig. 4.

---

[20] The semantics of Activities are based on a mathematical model of dynamic systems called *Petri Nets*, in case you are interested.

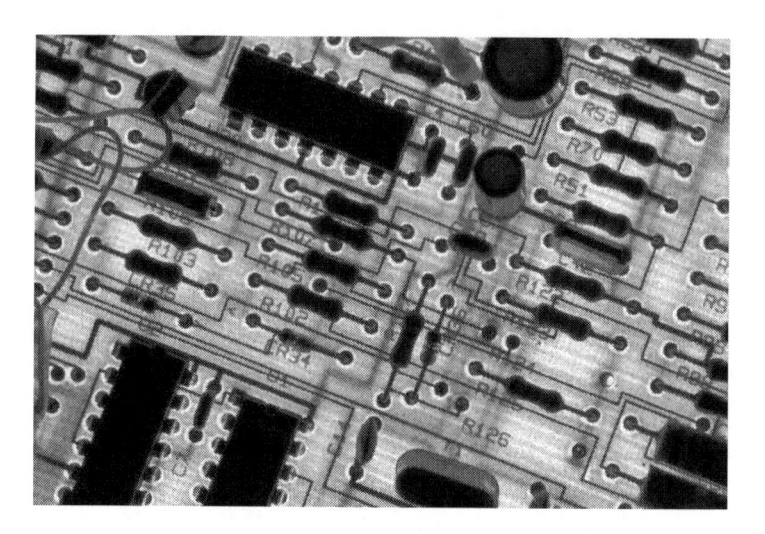

Figure 4: A circuit board as a metaphor for an Activity Diagram

This graphic illustrates quite nicely what is meant by the phrase 'graph of nodes' used in the definition above. An Activity will have a number of *executable nodes* (Actions), which are rather like the components on this circuit board, connected by *edges*, which are rather like the wires connecting the components. There are also *control nodes*, which affect the flow pathway.

In Fig. 5 is the set of node notations, presented in the Spec. The rounded corners of an Action node indicate it has behavior, the square corners of an Object node indicate it has no behavior.

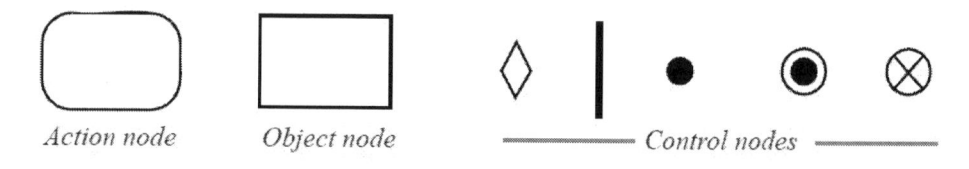

Action node   Object node   ————— Control nodes —————

Figure 5: Activity node notation [UML: Fig 15.4]

I will ignore Object nodes and Object flows for the time being, returning to them in chapters 8 and 9.

In Fig. 6 there is the Control Flow Edge notation. Control flows link Actions together in some way, typically as a sequence.

| Control flow (without actions) | Control flow edge linking two actions |

Figure 6: Activity Edge notation, Control Flows. [UML: Fig. 15.5]

5.2 A Business Process is a kind of Algorithm

A Business Process can be treated in many respects as an algorithm[21], and it turns out that any algorithm can be specified using only 3 logical building blocks types, which are: sequence, selection and iteration. Let us explore therefore the modeling of these 3 constructs in UML, using Activity Diagram notation, and focused on the specification of a Business Process.

5.3 Modeling Sequence

The simplest description of *sequence* for a Business Process would go something like: "Start – Do Some Work – Finish". How is this represented in an Activity?

An Activity is instantiated as the consequence of an event of some kind and the flow of control begins at a designated place, called the InitialNode. The first 'piece of work' in the Activity is done, modeled as an Action, and when that finishes, the next Action is activated, and then the next, and so on, until some kind of end is reached. Reaching the end is marked by an ActivityFinalNode.

In Fig. 7 there is an example of a sequence,[22] using an Activity Diagram, which models a very simplistic view for the moment of a recruitment Business Process.

---

[21] *"a process or set of rules to be followed in calculations or other problem-solving operations, especially by a computer". [Source: OED].*
[22] My tip to Business Process modellers, by the way, is to start the modelling of a Business Process with a simplistic 'Happy Path' view of the process being modelled, trying to summarise the work in the process into a sequence of between 5 to 9 steps initially. This helps to set out the basic structure of the process, from which further elaborations can be evolved.

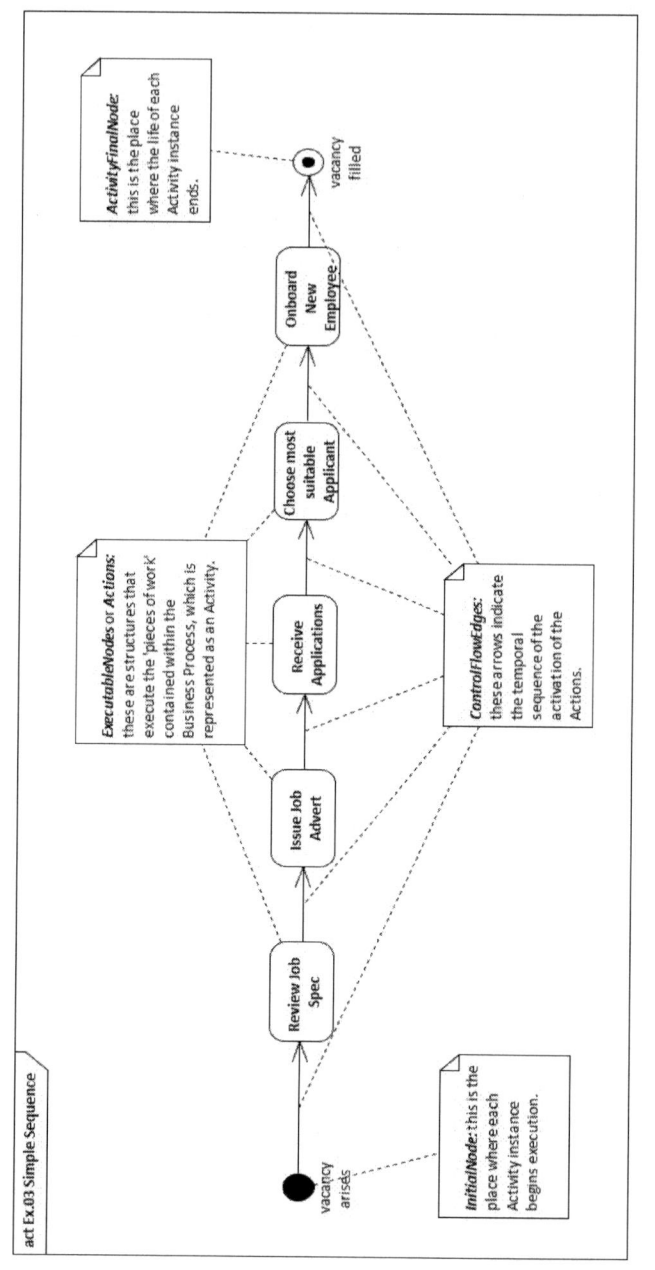

Figure 7: Activity as a simple sequence of Actions, depicting a Business Process as a sequence of Tasks

Let us deconstruct the diagram of Fig. 7 into the UML modeling elements used there:

-**Notes:** The comments in evidence on this diagram use the *Note* feature provided by UML. A Note can be placed on any diagram and linked to any element. Notes are very useful for communicating information to the diagram's audience, especially if we are just sketching, but it's important to appreciate that they don't have any semantic significance for the underlying Model. Hence their use does need to be governed by a Style Guide in situations where we wish to go beyond the sketching level of modeling.

-**Initial Node:** this type of ControlNode models the place where the Activity starts, once it has been instantiated. 'Instantiation' refers to the creation of an instance of the Activity by some structure. For the moment, in the case of Business Processes, we can just assume that the structure is the enterprise itself, or some function within it. In this example, every time a vacancy arises, which is the triggering event, a new instance of this Activity will be created. By default, each instance is independent of any other instance, so there could be several instances active at any one time, each trying to fill a different vacancy.

What we are modeling with an Activity therefore are all the possible behavior patterns which any particular instance could follow. This leads me to enunciate an important Activity modeling principle:

"the modeler must be clear as to what the instance of the Activity they are modeling represents in the real world."

An Activity will generally have only one InitialNode, especially in the context of Business Process modeling, although it could have more or none, something I will comment on later. An InitialNode cannot have any inbound Edges.

In Business Process modeling there is something of a convention to label the InitialNode with an event phrase indicative of the Business Event triggering the creation of the process instance; in this example *'vacancy arises'*. I believe this is useful information to show on this type of diagram, but I should emphasize that an InitialNode is a control node and *not* an event. By the time the

InitialNode is activated the event has already happened, so the use of this convention is something for the Style Guide to comment upon.

-**Activity Final Node**: this ControlNode indicates where the Activity instance will be finally extinguished; i.e. all the behavior of that instance will have been completed. Again the convention is to label this node with an event phrase, even though it is a control node; in the example '*vacancy filled*'.

There may be, and often are, many ActivityFinalNodes in an Activity modeling a Business Process, since it is common for processes to be able to end with distinct outcomes. The use of some kind of label is a way of visually distinguishing distinct end points, for the benefit of the audience.

An ActivityFinalNode cannot have any outbound Edges.

-**Executable Node**: an ExecutableNode is a node that is capable of performing behavior. There is only one type of ExecutableNode which is the Action. It is common, therefore, to refer to these nodes as simply Actions or Action nodes. Thus for example '*Review Job Spec*' is an Action node that invokes a behavior to review the Job Specification. Actions are conventionally labelled using verb-noun phrases, to emphasize that they 'do stuff'. Again the Style Guide should contain the naming conventions to be used.

The modeling approach taken here is to model the steps, or Tasks, in a Business Process as Actions. All the value-adding work carried out in a Business Process, which we model as an Activity, must be defined in terms of its Actions. Thus, each ExecutableNode is a placeholder in the Activity where some behavior takes place. On the whole, Actions in the context of Business Processes should produce effects, so it should be possible to say that something about the system's resources, or its environment, has changed as a result of invoking an Action. A tip I learnt a while ago in defining and assessing the validity of Tasks in a process, is to check that there is some *observable result* from the execution of each process Task. What significant thing *happened* as a result of the work? This trick also helps to come up with an appropriate label for the Task.

-**Control Flow Edge**: ControlFlows are Edges that show the 'flow of control' in the Activity from the InitialNode to the ActivityFinalNode(s).

When one Action finishes, the control flow arrow shows the next Action to be activated, if there is one; otherwise the flow is to the end of the Activity. Hence ControlFlows show the sequence of activation of the Actions in the Activity.

5.4 Modeling Selection

It is rare for a Business Process to be a strict sequence with only one path, so there will usually be a need to show significant selection points, where distinct paths may be followed. Fig. 8 is an example of 'selection' in our sample Business Process, showing the use of a DecisionControlNode to model a test, following the receipt of applications, to see if anyone has applied. The sequence pathway followed for any given instance of the Business Process is determined by the result of this test.

Also shown as fragments in the lower half of the diagram are a couple of alternative ways of showing the same DecisionControlNode logic. The fragment example on the left is quite common, and business friendly, especially if we are just sketching.

The fragment on the right, the «decisionInput», indicates the execution of a small routine to determine "are the number of applications > 0?". This style of notation would be appropriate at the implementer level of modeling. The modeler will decide the exact form of this, but the routine[23] here could be just a simple query behavior, possibly just reading the value of an Activity Variable, for example.

Because of these possible variations, the modeling team must adopt some standards concerning the labelling of DecisionControlNodes, and document this in their Style Guide.

The detailed rules concerning DecisionControlNodes in UML are surprisingly complex. However, their use overall is fairly intuitive, and when modeling Business Processes, it is important to bear in mind these simple rules:

- DecisionControlNodes route the process flow into distinct sequences, based on specified conditions, acting somewhat like points on a railway track.
- A DecisionControlNode should have exactly one inbound control flow and two or more outbound control flows.

---

[23] This type of routine is called a 'ValueSpecification' in UML. This modelling device has many uses in Activity modelling, as we shall see.

-All outbound control flows should have *guard conditions*, which are Boolean expressions that evaluate to *true* or *false*, shown in square brackets. These conditions should be mutually exclusive such that there is only ever one *true* outbound control flow that will be activated from the decision node, for any given Activity instance.

-The keyword *[else]* can be used on one of the outbound control flows. This is good practice as it ensures there is at least a default way out of a DecisionControlNode, if all the other guards evaluate to false.

-As mentioned above, a DecisionControlNode can access and manipulate information wherever that is stored to determine a result for the condition specified, but this must be simply 'read' behavior, with no side effects[24]. A DecisionControlNode (or in fact any ControlNode) can't change the state of anything significant in the Activity; only ActionNodes are allowed to do that. This is another way of saying that only ActionNodes do the real 'work' of the Activity.

5.5 Modeling Iteration

An iteration is a repeating cycle of steps in a process, based on some condition. There are three basic ways to include iteration in a UML Activity Diagram:

-Include a loop of ControlFlows, whereby Actions are invoked in an iterative fashion until some condition is met, controlled by a DecisionControlNode.

-Specify that an Action invokes an iterative behavior. There is no standard notation in UML to show this, but the detailed description of the Action's behavior could make this clear, as could the Action label.

-Use an ExpansionRegion, which I will discuss in a later chapter.

In the example of Fig. 9, the Action *'Receive Applications'* is intrinsically an iterative Action on the basis that many job applications could be received. The diagram doesn't have any special notation to indicate this, and actually it doesn't show the condition that would terminate the iteration – probably a time limit in this case. We will see later some different ways to introduce the time element into an Activity diagram, but, it any case, it's worth bearing in mind as a modeler that there will always be limits to what can be shown visually in any diagram.

---

[24] Such behaviors can derive *new* information provided it is based on information already available. For example the behaviour might evaluate a formula.

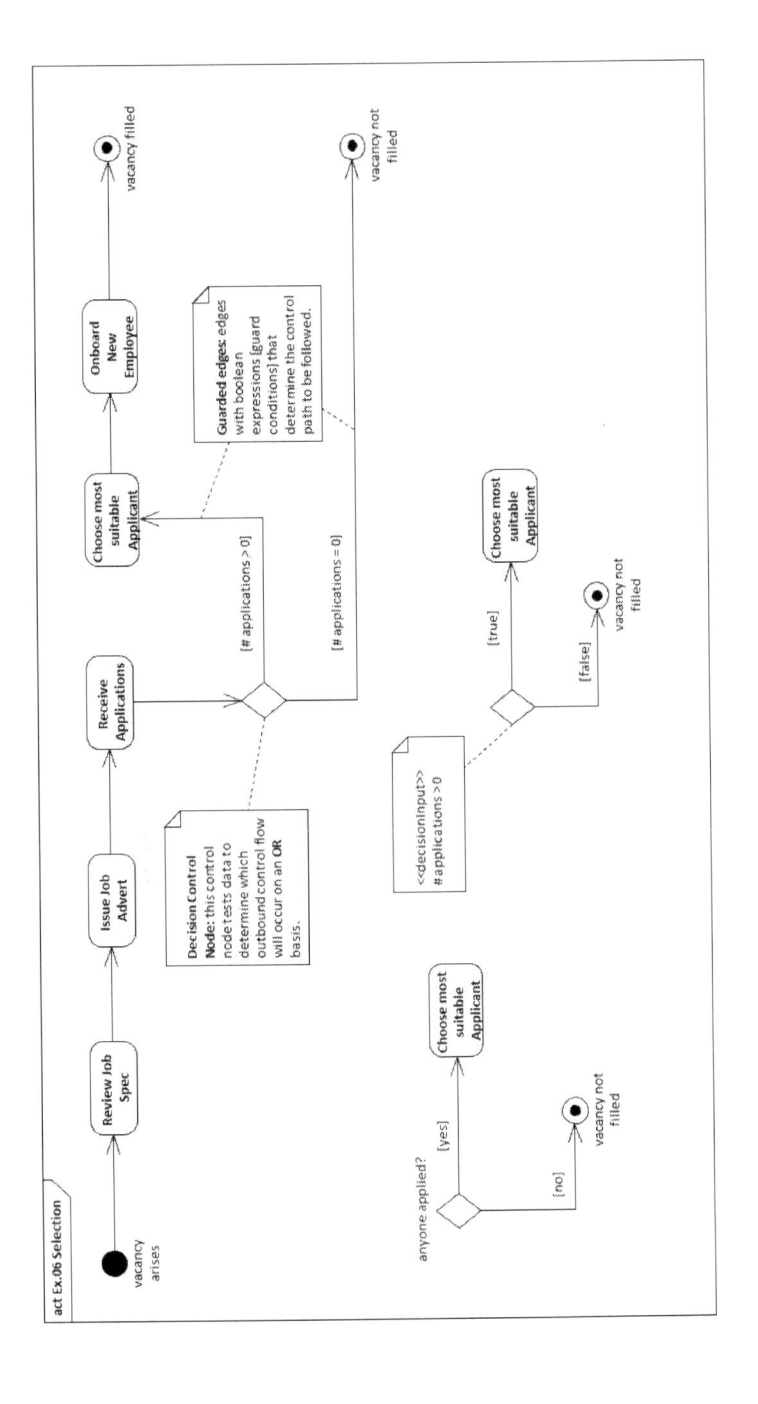

Figure 8: Example of an Activity Diagram showing Business Process 'selection'

Note that the Action *'Receive Applications'*, as shown in Figs. 7, 8 and 9, is possibly only ever invoked once; it is the logic of the behavior invoked by that Action that provides an iterative effect. However in the diagram of Fig. 9 it may be invoked more than once, since the business rules say that if no applications are received, a decision could be taken to re-issue an adjusted job advert (say with a bigger salary). Therefore another form of iteration is shown in Fig. 9, in the loop of Actions *'Receive Applications'*, *Review Job Advert'* and *'Issue Job Advert'*.

Fig. 9 also shows a new type of control node, the MergeControlNode. Merges merge two or more inbound control flows into a single outbound control flow.

The merge is needed because two or more control flows inbound to an Action directly have the sense of a logical AND. Without this merge in our example, the *'Issue Job Advert'* Action would have an inbound control flow from *'Review Job Spec'* **and** an inbound control flow from the *true* branch of the decision to re-issue. The effect of this is that *'Issue Job Advert'* would never be activated! To make it clear why this is so, I need to introduce the idea of *tokens* to you.

5.6 Tokens

To understand the logic behind how an Activity really works, it is useful to think that there are one or more imaginary *tokens* flowing through the diagram, rather as an electron might flow through the circuit board that we used as a metaphor earlier in this chapter.

In the simple sequence example we started with above, Fig. 7, when the Activity starts we imagine a control token is placed on the InitialNode, and immediately flows along the ControlFlow to the first Action, *'Review Job Spec'*, and activates it. When the *'Review Job Spec'* Action finishes, the token passes on to the next Action, *'Issue Job Advert'* and so on successively until the token reaches the ActivityFinalNode, which 'swallows it up', and the Activity instance ends. So the token is tracing out a pathway through the Activity, from beginning to end.

It might help to think of a token as a locomotive moving along a railway system. The Actions are like stations on the way, which the locomotive arrives at. The locomotive arrival provokes behaviors like 'getting off' and 'getting on' etc.

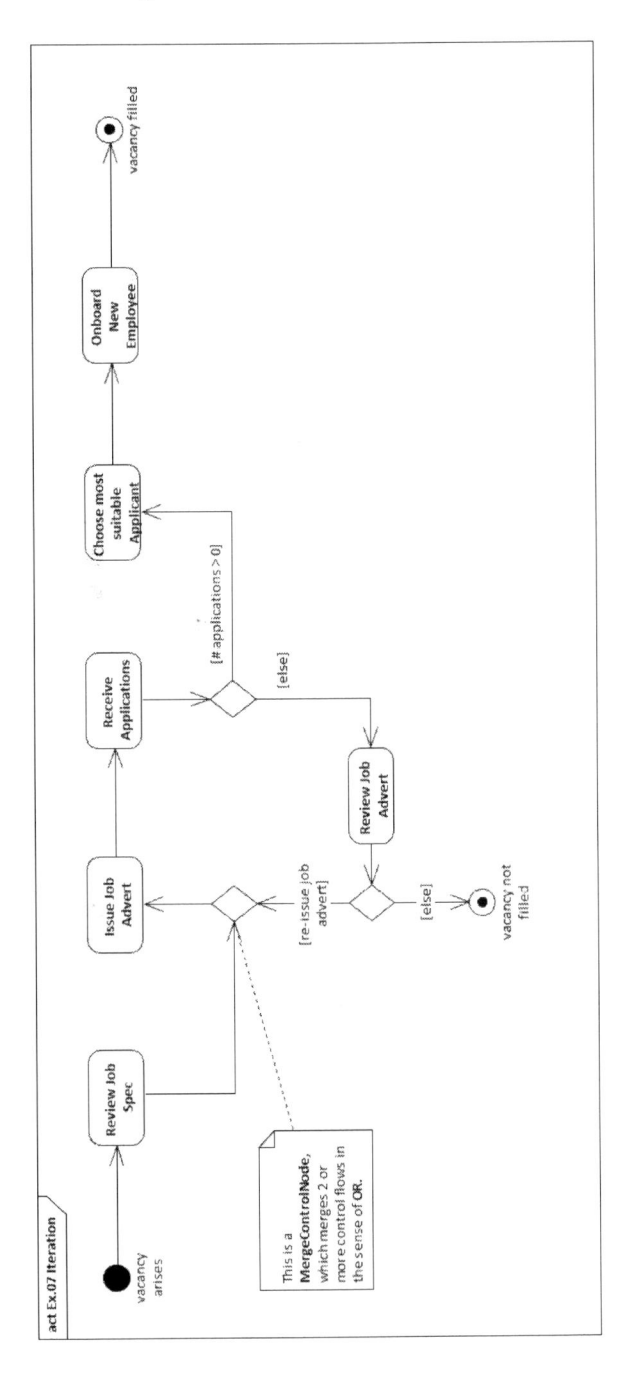

Figure 9: Example of iteration in Activities that model Business Processes

In the selection example we saw above, Fig. 8, when the token reaches the DecisionControlNode, it can be routed either one way or another, depending on the result of the data test indicated. In either case it will eventually end up at an ActivityFinalNode, be consumed and the Activity instance will terminate. So ControlNodes are rather like points on the railway tracks, which direct the locomotive to go one way or another.

In the third example showing iteration, Fig. 9, the token's movements are potentially more complicated. Actually all is well because we have the MergeControlNode, but let's suppose we had drawn the diagram in the way shown in Fig. 10 instead, omitting the merge.

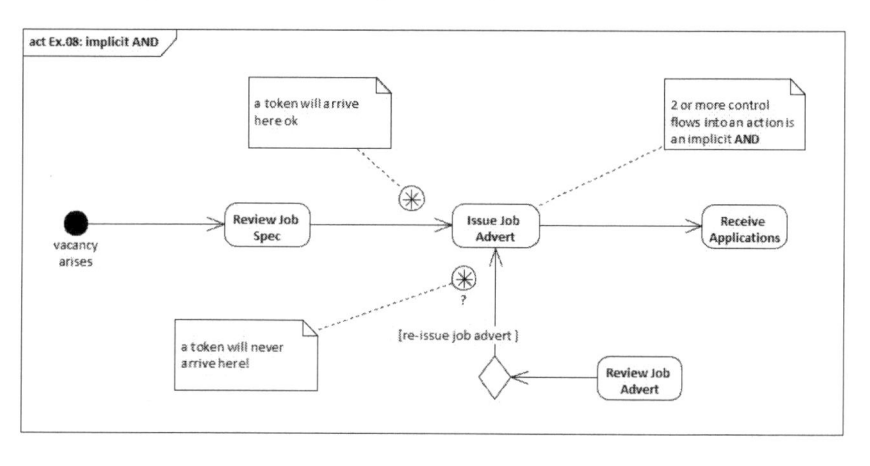

Figure 10: Fragment showing an implicit AND

In the fragment of Fig. 10, the Action *Issue Job Advert* now has two inbound control flows, and the UML rules say that a token must be present on *both* flows for the Action to activate[25]. So if a token arrives on one ControlFlow, the Action has to wait for a token to arrive on the other flow in order to activate. But this will never happen in the diagram fragment of Fig. 10; the token will arrive at *Issue Job Advert* from *Review Job Spec* ok, but now the Activity is 'stuck' there waiting for another token, from *Review Job Advert*, which will never arrive, since in this Activity there is just one token moving around.

Using the MergeControlNode solves this problem, since in that case *Issue Job Advert* has only one inbound control flow, which the single token can reach by two different paths. Convince yourself by tracing out all the possible pathways that the token could take in Fig. 9, before reaching an

---

[25] This is due to the logic of Petri nets. Personally, I think this is a real nuisance. In other notations, notably BPMN, two or more inbound flows to a Task would be treated as an implicit OR.

ActivityFinalNode.

A top tip for drawing Activity Diagrams accurately is to 'account for the tokens'[26]. Accounting for tokens means understanding where they are created, how they move around and how they are eventually consumed. The understanding of token flow is essential for creating accurate UML Activities and also for delving deeper into their use, so it is worth taking a moment or two to assimilate this topic thoroughly.

The logic of token flow can be leveraged to do useful things like error checking and simulations in the more powerful modeling tools. This is so the modeler can get a sense of how the process based on their model would perform in BaU. UML regards Activities as 'virtual machines', whose behavior is fully described by these token flows.

There are in fact two types of token to help us shape an Activity: control tokens and object tokens. I am only dealing with control tokens here, as I will be discussing the use of object tokens in chapters 8 and 9.

5.7 Explicit AND Logic

It is possible, and frequently the case, that a sequence flow in a Business Process splits at some point into two or more 'parallel' flows. 'Parallel' means that the Tasks in one flow are independent of the Tasks in any other parallel flow, so that they could execute concurrently or in any order. As usual an example makes this feature clearer.

In the Business Process modeled in Fig. 12 once a successful candidate has been selected, they are onboarded, and regret letters are sent to unsuccessful candidates. There is no reason to do this in any particular order, so we can represent this as parallel sequences. Note that 'parallel' doesn't mean strictly 'at the same time'; the business could do the Tasks of one flow before the other or they could overlap in time.

The ForkControlNode is the control symbol that indicates the start of parallel sequences. When a control token reaches a Fork, it splits into a number of new tokens, one for each outbound flow. Each of these tokens then proceeds independently according to the logic of that particular sequence. So in our example a token activates *'Onboard New Employee'* and another token activates *'Send Regret Letters'*.

The JoinControlNode merges the sequences back together again in the sense of a logical AND. A Join holds any tokens that arrive at it, until all the

---

[26] This is obviously less important at the sketching level of modeling.

tokens due, one for each of its inbound flows, have arrived. It then merges them all into a single token to pass onto its single outbound flow.

Note that a Join doesn't *have to* follow every Fork – it just depends on the logic of the process. But it *is* necessary to make sure that all tokens generated can reach an ActivityFinalNode, because the Activity instance does not end until all the active tokens are consumed in some way. We will see later that there are some mechanisms other than ActivityFinalNodes, which also deal with consuming or abandoning tokens in some way.

5.8 Implicit Forks and Joins

The diagram in Fig. 11 illustrates the potential for using implicit Forks and Joins – notice the 'bar' control symbol is not used.

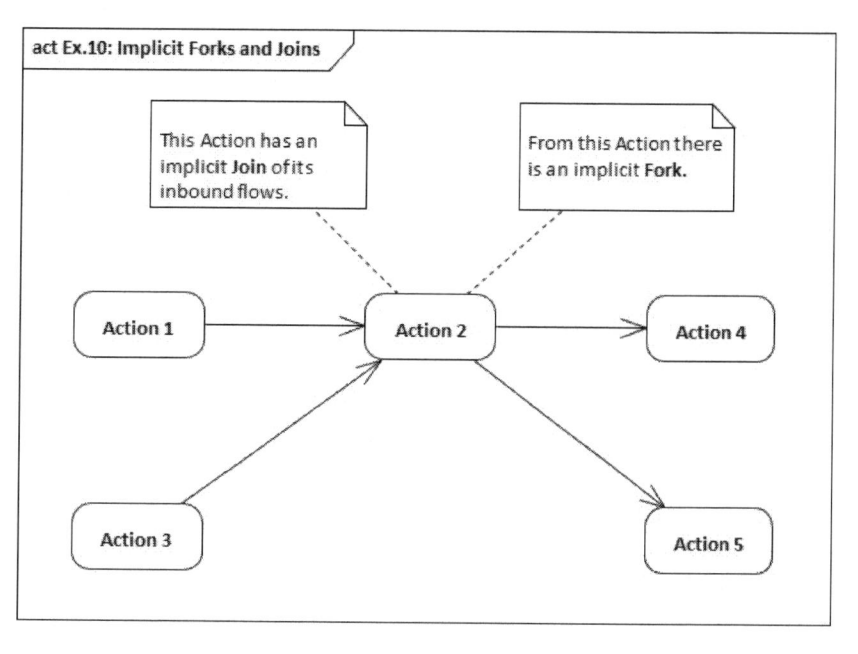

Figure 11: Illustration of Implicit Forks and Joins

There will be cases where explicit Forks and Joins are needed, but the diagram 'clutter' might be reduced by using implicit ones where they are appropriate. This is a matter for the modeler to decide, and there should be guidance on this in the Style Guide.

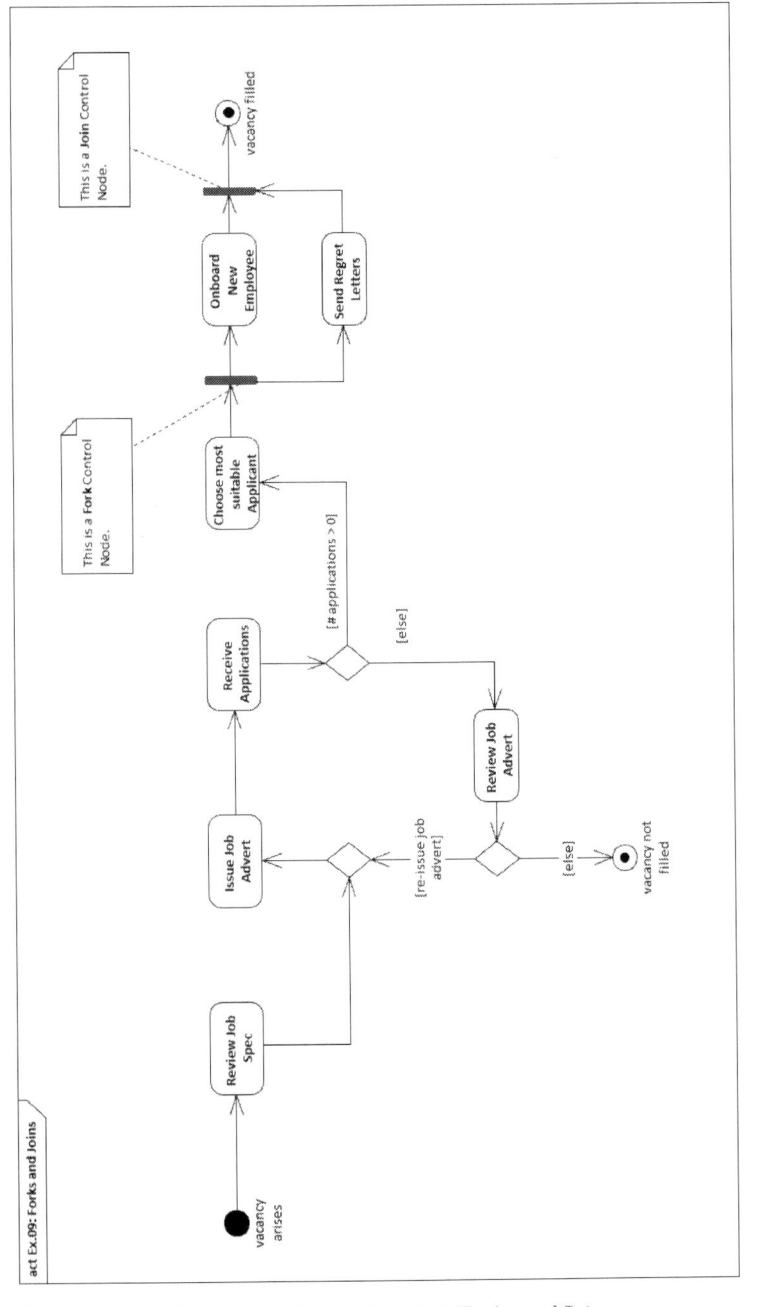

Figure 12: Activity showing the use of explicit Forks and Joins

5.9 Conclusion

With the knowledge you have gained in this chapter you will be able to model a large percentage of Business Process logic encountered in real situations, certainly at the sketching level. The next chapter deals with some of the more subtle issues that might arise in real Business Processes, and shows you how to model them using UML Activity features. This shifts the Handbook's review of Activities more towards the blueprint level of modeling.

6. BEYOND THE ELEMENTARY NOTATION

An exposition of Activity elements and Business Process logic that might not be considered elementary.

There are a number of modeling challenges that might arise, as we try to capture the specification of a Business Process, where the modeler might make good use of additional modeling elements made available to us as part of the UML Activity specification.

6.1 Flow Final Node

Whenever any token reaches an ActivityFinalNode, the entire Activity instance is extinguished, *even if* there are other tokens still active in other parts of the Activity. It's a sort of 'sudden death' node, the 'terminator'.

Consider the Activity Diagram fragments in Fig. 13.

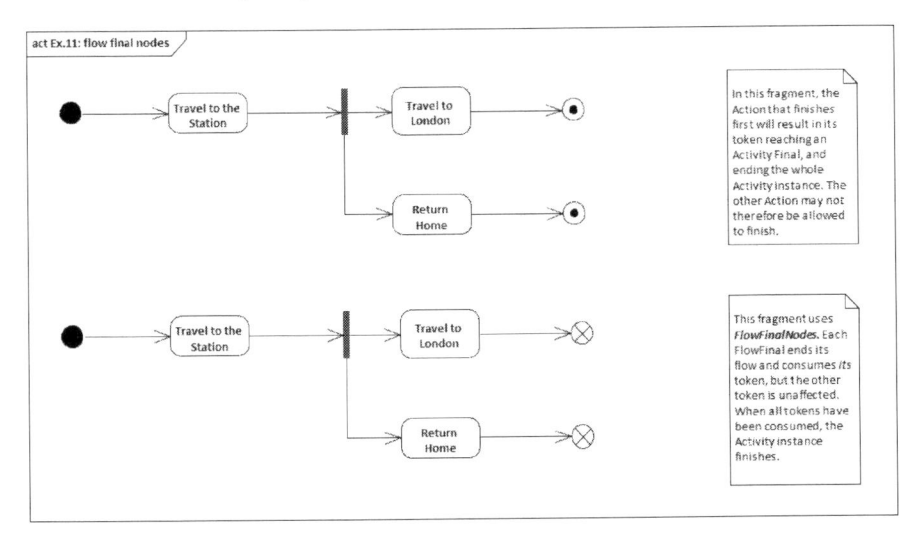

Figure 13: Use of ActivityFinalNodes *vs.* FlowFinalNodes

In this example, we imagine that I travel to the train station with my partner. She drops me off and I catch the train to London for a meeting. Meanwhile she returns home, as she is working from home that day.

Both of these Actions should be allowed to complete before the Activity instance terminates. However, in the top example, which uses ActivityFinalNodes, whichever of the two tokens from the Fork reaches an ActivityFinalNode first, its arrival will end the whole Activity instance, *even though* the other token is still active.

37

The use of FlowFinalNodes in the lower fragment solve this problem because a FlowFinalNode will consume any token that arrives there, but other tokens elsewhere are not affected. If only FlowFinals are used, the Activity instance is extinguished only when all active tokens have been consumed.[27]

One consequence of this is that it is possible to create an Activity Diagram with no ActivityFinalNodes. Also, it is quite common to see a mixture of FlowFinals and ActivityFinals.

While we are on the subject of the dangers of ActivityFinalNodes, be aware of a 'gotcha' that catches many folk out. You might reasonably expect that two control flows *into* an ActivityFinalNode would be an implicit AND, of the sort we have seen previously with Actions. But it isn't! Any token reaching any ActivityFinalNode at any time means the whole Activity instance finishes at that point. The ActivityFinalNode won't wait for any other possible token to arrive[28].

6.2 Signals and Messages

Signals are a type of ActionNode that sends or receives messages[29] or signals asynchronously. It is customary to think of a 'message' as targeted at a specific recipient, whereas a 'signal' is some form of broadcast. Asynchronous means the message or signal is sent, but the sender does not wait for a reply. Formally UML calls these Actions SendSignalAction and AcceptEventAction, but in the context of Business Processes I prefer to call these Actions simply SendSignal and ReceiveSignal.

Signals are a widely accepted way of modeling the generation and recognition of Business Events within Activities. A SendSignal can be used to model sending a message that is targeted at a specific receptor, such as a Customer, or it could be used to model a signal broadcast to a group of receptors. In the latter case the specific receptors may be unknown to the process, rather like a radio broadcast[30]. A striking and well-known example of this type of signal is the white smoke that emerges from the Vatican chimney when a new Pope has been elected.

---

[27] At least in this case, the same effect could have been achieved by modeling a Join, but that might be less convenient to draw and maintain.

[28] As a general rule ControlNodes can't store tokens. The exceptions are Joins, and InitialNodes where there is a guard condition on the outbound ControlFlow.

[29] In this section I will discuss signals in terms of information passing, but note that the sending or receiving of physical objects can be modeled in the same way.

[30] In UML there is no notational difference between sending a message, which is targeted, and broadcasting a signal, which may not be targeted. However the distinction can be made in the definition of the type of Signal Action which sits in the Model.

A **ReceiveSignal** is an Action node where the Activity will wait for a message or signal to arrive before proceeding. The wait occurs when a token reaches the **ReceiveSignal** to activate it. Note that the passage of any other tokens elsewhere in the Activity are not affected by the wait.

In terms of using these nodes in Business Process modeling, sending and receiving signals is generally used to communicate with some entity considered external to the process[31]. The modeler has the choice of deciding which entities are considered internal and which external; 'external' does not necessarily mean external to the enterprise.

Internal entities are actors that execute Tasks within the process specification. As we will see later they can be included in Activity Diagrams as **Partitions**. External entities don't execute Tasks within the process specification, but do communicate, via messages, with the process for some reason.

Accept event action   *Accept time event action*

Figure 14: Notation for sending and receiving Signals [UML: Fig.16.18 and Fig.16.40]

The 'egg timer' symbol shown in Fig. 14 is a special case of the **ReceiveSignal**. This may be used where we wish to show the influence of a time event on a process (as it were, 'receiving' a time signal). It is customary to refer to this type of Action informally as a 'Timer'.

In Fig. 15 there is an example of the use of these additional elements, modifying an earlier diagram. These modifications get the Model closer to the reality of the Business Process and convey more detailed information to the diagram's audience.

---

[31] Internal communication is possible too, but much rarer. I will show an example of this in a later chapter.

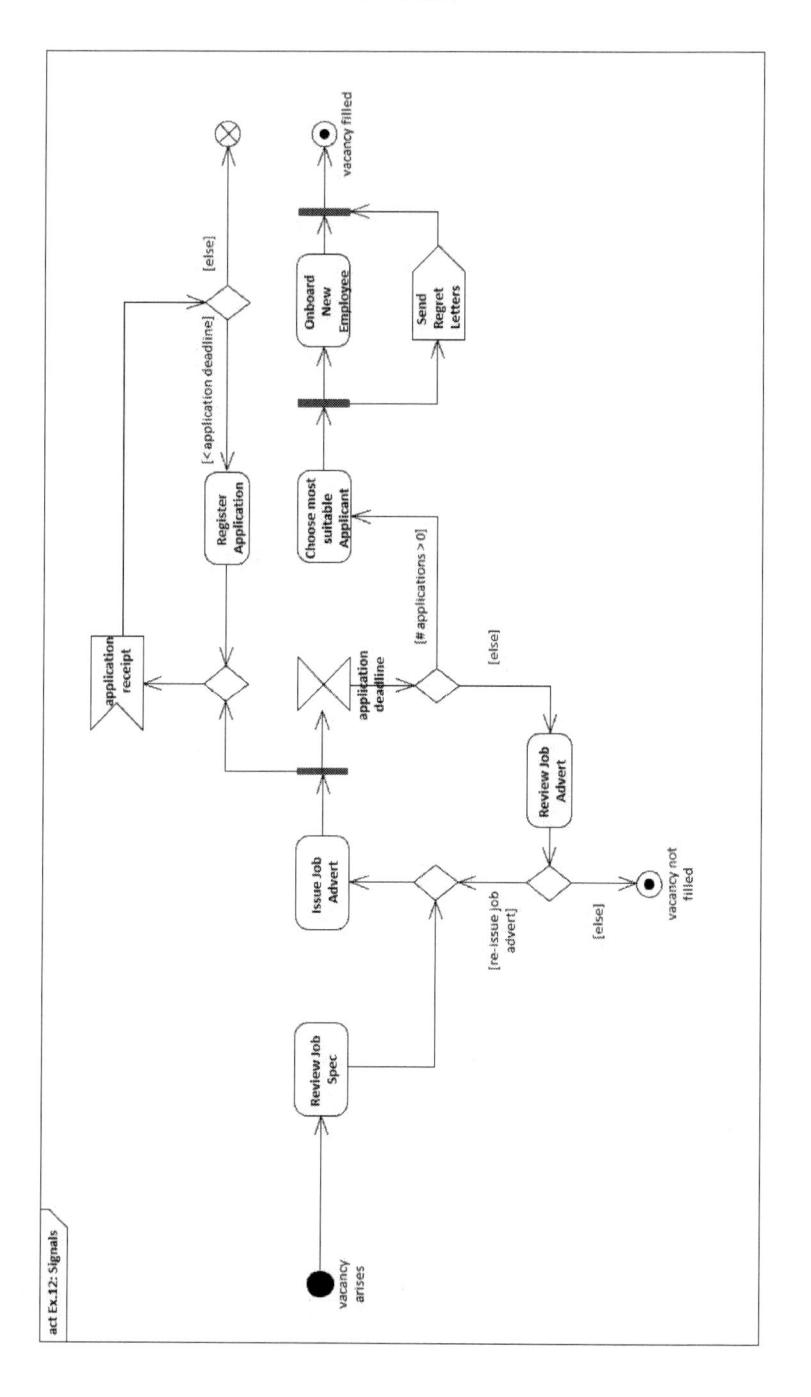

Figure 15: Illustration of the use of Signals

The modifications from the previous version of this diagram, Fig. 12, are as follows:

-A Fork has been added, to model the process more accurately, now that we know about the use of signals. After the new Fork, one token is sent to activate a ReceiveSignal which receives job applications sent in, which are then registered. Another token is sent to activate a Timer, to wait for the job application date deadline to be reached. We need this Timer because there may not be any applications at all, in which case the Activity will be stuck at the ReceiveSignal forever! As soon as the deadline date arrives the Timer's token will automatically move on, along the outbound control flow.

You can see that a loop has been set up around the signal *'application receipt'*. This is needed because as soon as any job application is received the token will flow away from the signal and the signal will therefore no longer be active. Hence we need to route the token back to *re-activate* the ReceiveSignal after each application receipt, until the deadline is reached. If the signal is not active, it can't receive applications.

We have to be a little bit careful with this signal token. The way this is set up, there will be a token on the ReceiveSignal after the deadline has passed, so we need to make sure it is accounted for. If there were no applications at all, or none after the deadline, one of the ActivityFinalNodes will eventually get rid of it. If an application comes in after the deadline, we simply don't re-activate the signal, and the token will be consumed by the FlowFinalNode shown.

-The Action to *'Send Regret Letters'* is now modelled as a SendSignal, since these will be sent to the unsuccessful applicants who are considered external to the process. The documentation of this Action in the Model would need to make clear that the Action processes a group of objects. Another option here would be to use an ExpansionRegion, which is a node type I will discuss in a later chapter.

6.3 Interruptible Activity Regions

Actions enclosed in an InterruptibleActivityRegion can be collectively aborted if a specified event occurs.

Fig. 16 is an example of the use of an InterruptibleActivityRegion, which is indicated visually by a rectangle with a dashed border. After activating the

Action *'Issue Job Advert'*, a token passes into an InterruptibleActivityRegion, which may be labelled. This activates a ReceiveSignal *'recruitment cancelled'* and another token is placed there. While the original token is still inside the region, if a signal cancelling the recruitment is received, the original token is abandoned, and a new flow occurs from the cancellation signal to the SendSignal *'Inform any Applicants'*. However once the original token leaves the region, the cancellation signal is no longer active, and its token is abandoned. The signal can no longer be triggered by a message, even if one arrives (i.e. it's no longer 'listening').

The InterruptibleActivityRegion modeling device is useful in general for those circumstances where a message may be received at any time outside of the normal flow of the process, and the arrival of that message should abort a specified portion of the Activity. The scope of a region will depend upon the business rules, and there may be more than one region, as many as required.

The 'lightening arrow' shaped Edge that appears in the diagram is called an InterruptingEdge, and models the occurrence of an exception flow in general terms. I will discuss UML exceptions in more detail in a later chapter.

It is also possible that we need to model situations where the arrival of a message or signal occurs outside of the main process flow, and must be dealt with, but it should *not* abort the main flow of the Activity. That is, we need a way to generate an *additional* flow. I will deal with that possibility next.

6.4 Non-interrupting additional flows

Situations may arise in Business Processes whereby, during the normal execution of the process, certain messages or signals must be dealt with *concurrently* with the main flow, and therefore their processing should not interrupt or abort the main flow.

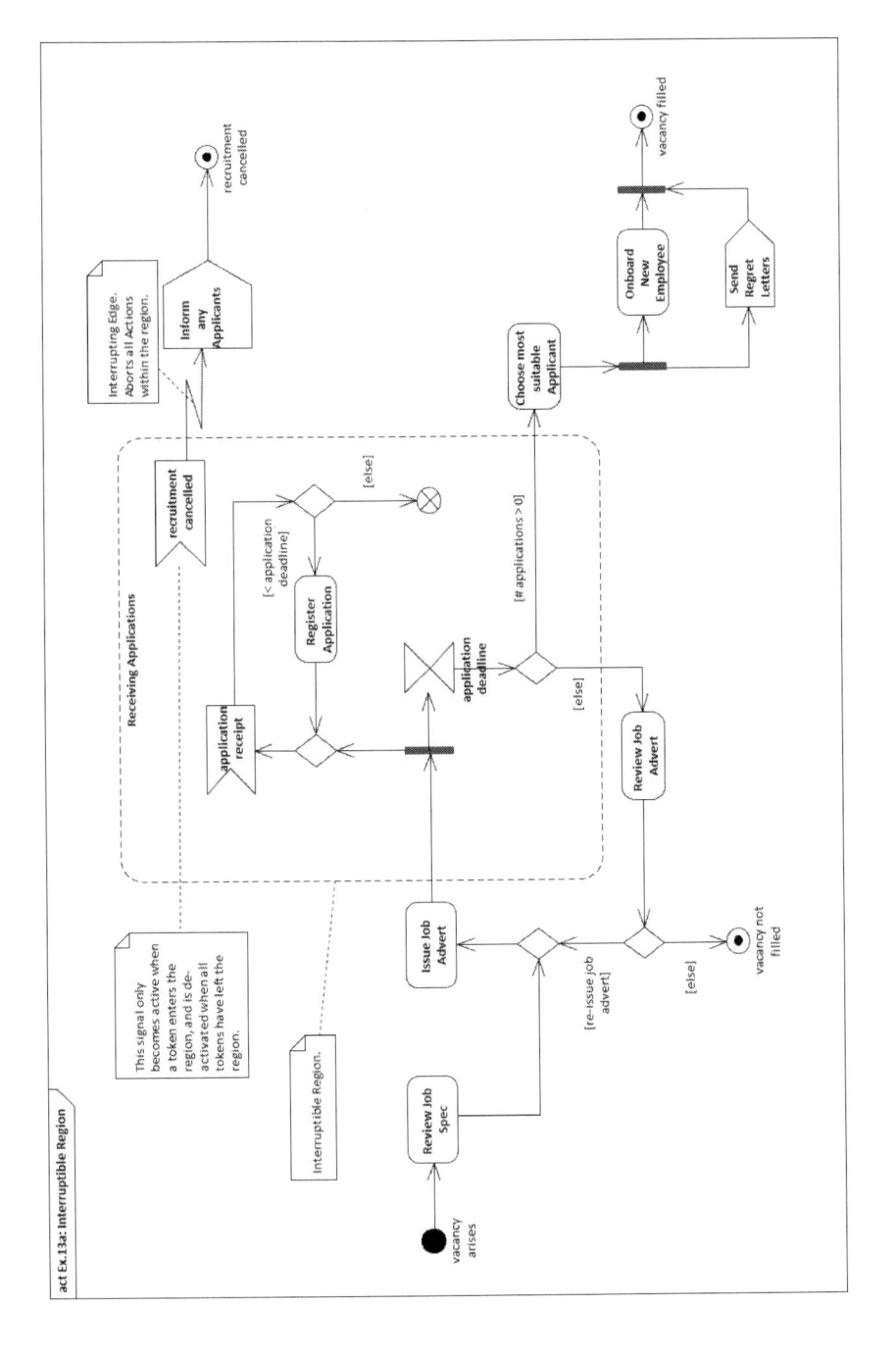

Figure 16: Example use of InterruptibleActivityRegion

There is an example of this in Fig. 17. The ReceiveSignal *'new employment benefit'* is enabled as soon as the Activity instance is created, and a token is placed there. The UML rules state that any Action node that does not have an inbound control flow, is active with its own token as soon as the Activity instance is created. If the *'new employment benefit'* event does occur, the token will activate the Action *'Update Job Spec'* and then flow to the FlowFinalNode shown, where it will be consumed. This flow does not interrupt the main flow, and proceeds in parallel with the main flow.

The interesting thing is that a new token is placed on this ReceiveSignal *after every activation*, so if the event occurs again the signal will be processed again, as many times as necessary. The main flow token reaching an ActivityFinalNode will kill off the token that is always present at this signal.

These flows certainly look odd when you encounter them for the first time, because they appear to be somehow 'hanging', disconnected from the main sequence flow. There can be as many of these sorts of flows as required, or of course, none at all.

I also made another change in Fig. 17 from the previous version, Fig. 16. Now we know about the semantics of ReceiveSignals with no inbound flows, and we know about InterruptibleActivityRegions we can combine these ideas to make a simpler model. The ReceiveSignal to receive applications only needs to be active once the Activity flow enters the InterruptibleActivityRegion. If we model this signal with no inbound flow, then it will be activated only when the main token enters the region and it will be deactivated when the main token leaves the region.[32] This avoids us having to worry about that pesky token that is always sitting on the *'application receipt'* signal.

6.5 Actions which invoke Activities

When engaged in Business Process modeling it is important to have a strategy for dealing with complexity. To this end modelers often use a few distinct levels of process modeling, something I alluded to in an earlier chapter.

---

[32] This is a reasonable interpretation, but the Spec doesn't actually make this clear. The signal attached to the interrupting edge will certainly be de-activated because of the semantics of exceptions.

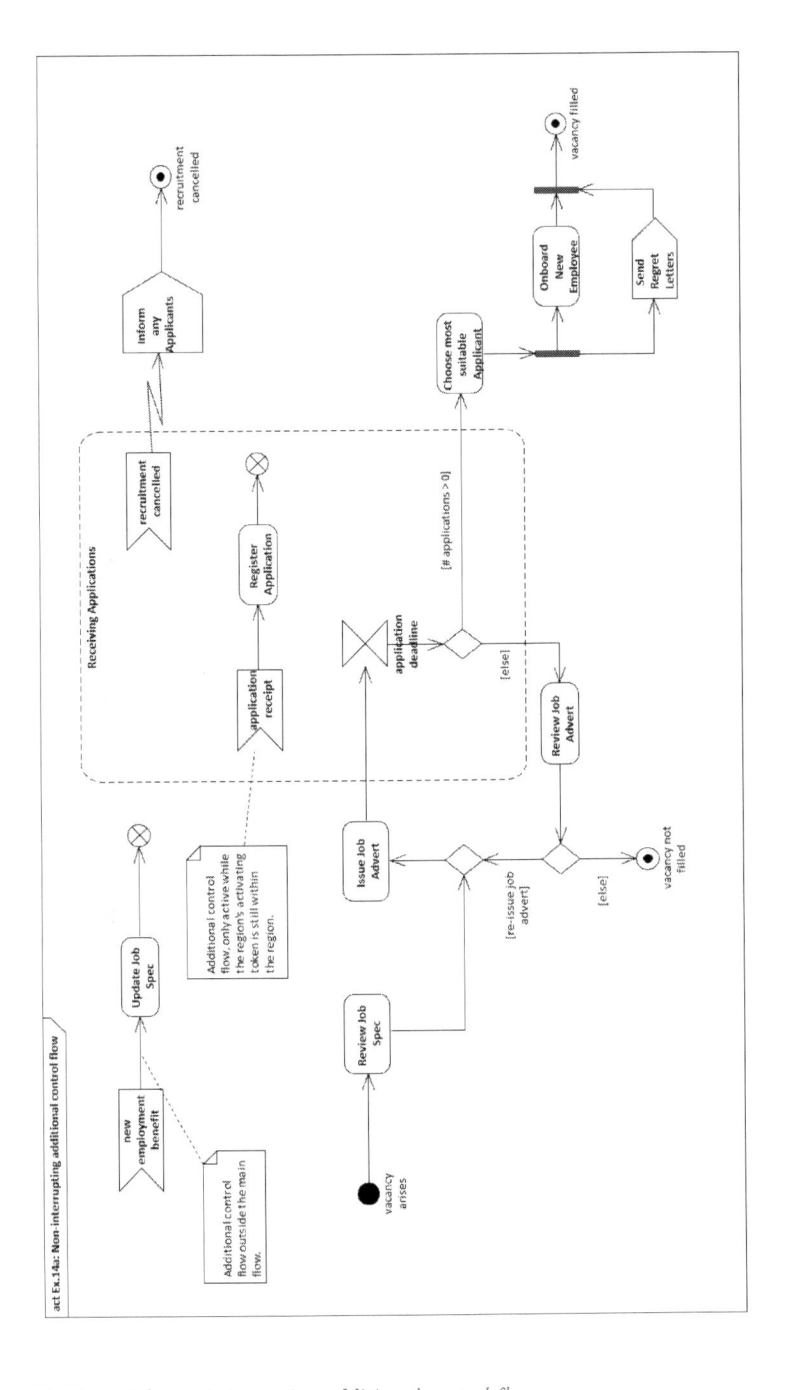

Figure 17: Example non-interrupting additional control flow

In particular the first level of modeling of a Business Process at Level 2 is often modelled as a collection of *Sub-Processes*, with each Sub-Process the subject of its own diagram. We can model this approach using UML Activity Diagrams, by designating an Action as a *CallBehavior* type which means that the Action will invoke a 'child' Activity, which has its own diagram and Model features.

The notation for this is a 'rake-like' symbol, as shown in Fig. 18, meant to depict a hierarchy.

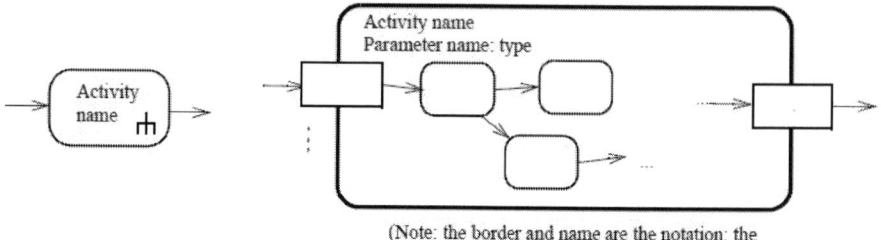

(Note: the border and name are the notation; the other symbols are present to provide clarity, only.)

Figure 18: Action which invokes an Activity. [UML Fig 16.5]

In the main, 'parent', Activity diagram, the Action itself can look normal enough except for the rake symbol. However, the 'child' Activity that is the Sub-Process could also be shown expanded inside the Action, as shown in Fig. 18. A decent tool would allow this expansion and contraction to be shown easily at will. Another option is for the tool to hyperlink the parent diagram with its child diagram(s) in some simple and effective way.

In all respects the Action that invokes an Activity obeys the same semantic rules as any other Action as far as the parent diagram is concerned. Also the child diagram obeys all of the Activity Diagram semantics we have discussed in this Handbook so far. However, note that reaching an ActivityFinalNode in the child diagram indicates the extinction of the instance of the child Activity, but that does *not* extinguish the parent Activity instance.

Supposing there could well be distinct results from the execution of a child Activity, the result of what happened there could be tested by a control node in the parent diagram. This is possible because parent-level data could be made available to the child, for example via parameters that pass data into and out of any Action or Activity. I will discuss parameters and data flow in more detail in a later chapter.

In Fig. 19, there is an illustration of this, where I designate the Action

'Onboard New Employee', as a child Activity. My first step is to change the definition of the Action in the parent diagram, for example the one in Fig. 18, to be a *CallBehavior* type, which should produce the 'rake' symbol in the parent diagram. I then create the child Activity Diagram, using the tool facilities available. Finally in the parent diagram I could insert a DecisionControlNode to test whether the onboarding Action was successful or not, and act accordingly.

Note I have designated the child Activity's Action 'Perform Induction Activity' as a *CallBehavior* type also, so that Action would be the subject of yet another level of diagramming. There is no limit to the number of levels in such a hierarchy, but in practice it is rare to need more than three levels of process modeling at Level 2, before reaching the atomic Task level.

Although this is not shown in the examples, it is fairly common to model the first level of a Business Process description with all the Actions designated as *CallBehaviours*. This is desirable in order to manage complexity effectively. A good rule of thumb in this regard is to try to summarize the process work at any given level into 7+/- 2 'pieces', until the atomic Task level is reached. This guidance could be mentioned in the Style Guide.

6.6 Partitions

Partitions are a way of grouping Actions together based on some interesting criteria. In Business Process modeling, often the grouping shows roles, actors or organization units responsible for performing the Tasks, but for example they might show geographical locations or even IT systems.

Note that the use of Partitions does not affect the token flow logic of the Activity in any way, but they do make it clear which entities host, or could/should host, the behaviors defined in the Activity. This information is very useful for the development of both Business Architectures and IT systems specifications.

The notation for Partitions is shown in Fig. 20, which shows that Partitions can be nested and Actions can be classified simultaneously in different ways (although this could be awkward to show diagrammatically). The 'top level' of any given classification is called a 'dimension', for example 'Location' or 'Organization Unit'. A dimension (Partition property *isDimension*), may not be part of another dimension. [UML: §15.6.3.1].

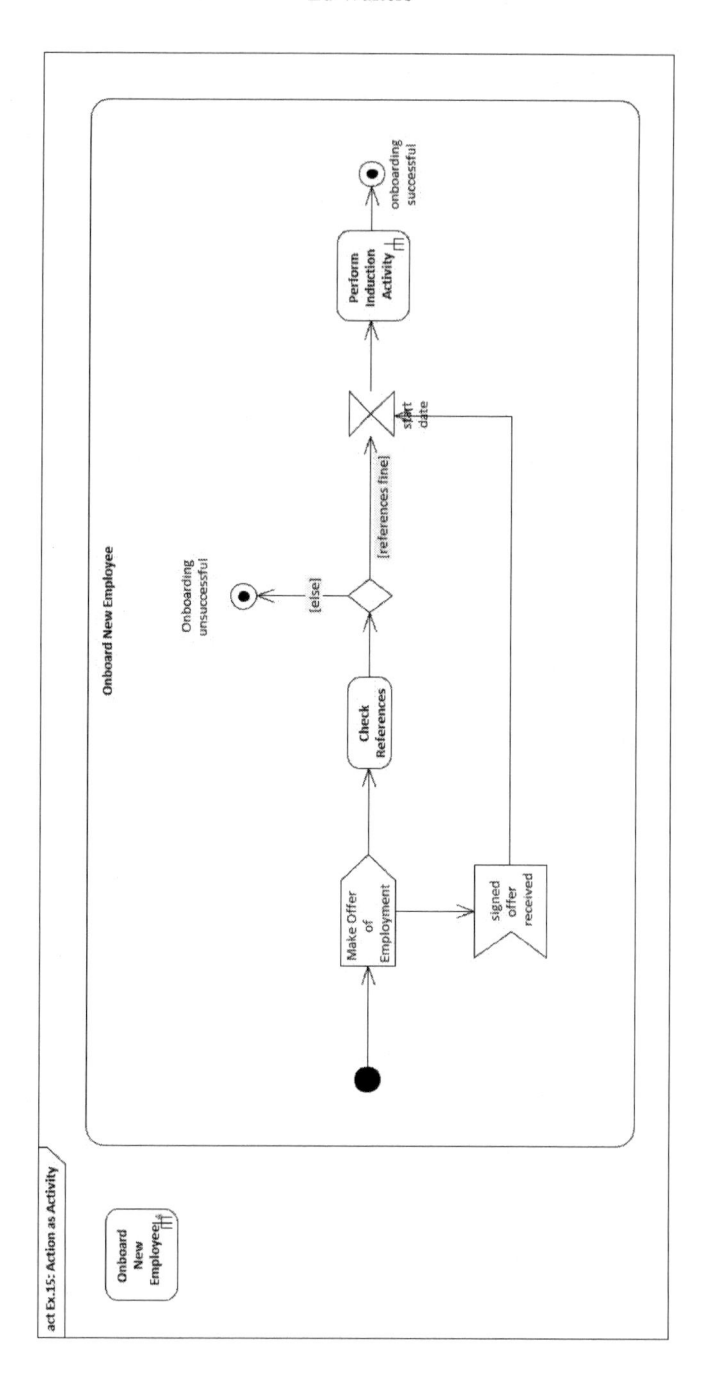

Figure 19: Example of a CallBehaviour Action and a 'child' Activity Diagram

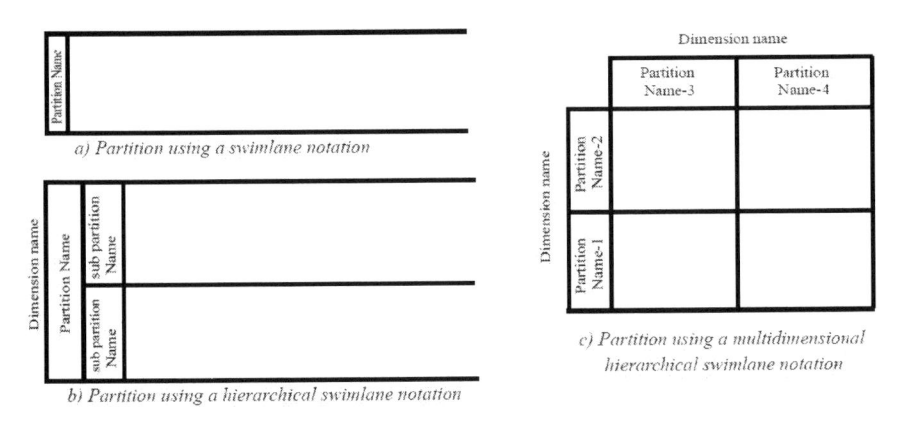

Figure 20: **Partition** *notation [UML: Fig. 15.66]*

It is also possible to show **Partitions** as a label on the Action, rather than use the 'swimlane' notation. See Fig. 21.

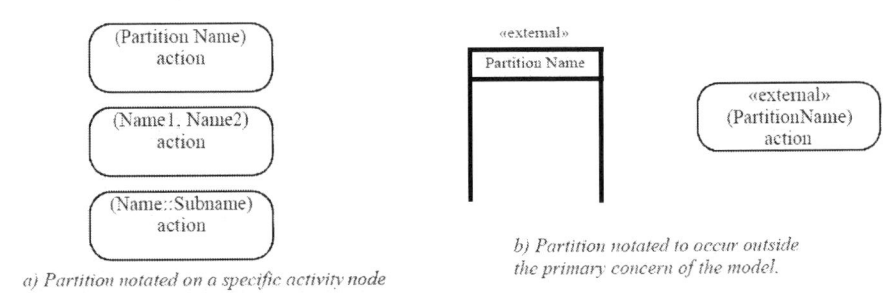

Figure 21: Annotating **Partitions** *on the Action itself [UML: Fig.15.67]*

Notice that the Spec mentions the possibility of using **Partitions** to indicate external entities, using the notation shown in Fig. 21. However this would not be considered best practice in Business Process modeling, since the main reason for designating an entity as 'external' is that we don't really know what Actions they actually perform, nor do we control the resources involved. In the contemporary style of process modeling, we generally model the communications with external entities via signals, which are messages between 'our' process and 'theirs'. These exchanges will be the subject of an appropriate protocol between peer organizations.

6.7 Compound Control Nodes

If a MergeControlNode is followed immediately by a DecisionControlNode, or vice versa, it is permitted to use a single notational symbol. The same applies to ForkControlNodes and JoinControlNodes.

Although this does reduce the number of symbols in the diagram, it may make the diagram harder to interpret. I personally discourage this usage, but in any case the Style Guide must address whether their use is to be permitted or discouraged.

Fig. 22 and 23 are reproduced from the Spec.

Merge node and decision node used together, sharing the same symbol

Figure 22: Notation for combined Merge and Decision nodes [UML: Fig. 15.34]

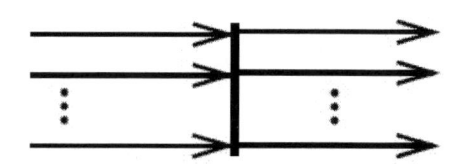

Join node and fork node used together, sharing the same symbol

Figure 23: Notation for combined Fork and Join [UML: Fig.15.31]

6.8 Guard Conditions on Control Flows

Any control flow (in fact any Activity **Edge**) can have a guard condition attached to it. So far we have only seen this in the context of **DecisionControlNodes**. Recall that the guard must evaluate to *true*, before the token flow can occur across the **Edge**.

One additional and fairly common use of guard conditions on **ControlFlows**, is associated with **ForkControlNodes**. The control flows from Forks we have seen so far have been unconditional. But imagine a situation, where a Fork may produce one or more parallel flows, depending on individual conditions associated with each possible flow.

An example is shown in Fig. 24. This arrangement is sometimes called (but not in UML) an IOR control (inclusive OR) or an AND/OR control.

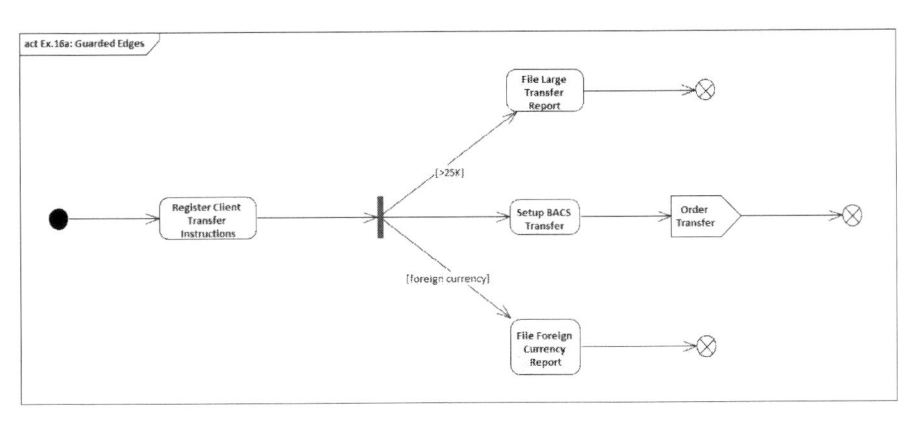

Figure 24: Guarded Edges from Forks

In Fig. 24, there are two guarded control flows from the ForkControlNode. This means that from this Fork there could 1 *or* 2 *or* 3 control flows, depending on which guard conditions evaluate to *true*.

Be aware though that there's another potential 'gotcha' here to trap the unwary. Notice that I didn't use a Join to synchronise these flows, because there is no guarantee that 3 tokens would always arrive at it, which could mean the Activity is 'stuck' at the Join, unable to finish. A Join *always* expects a token on *each* inbound flow, so the Activity instance will wait there forever, if they can't arrive[33].

Given this logic, it's worth mentioning the importance of ensuring that there is at least one *unguarded* control flow outbound from a Fork, so that there is always at least one downstream flow away from it. This requirement should be included in the Style Guide. The keyword *[else]* obviously can't be used here, because conditions on flows from a Fork won't be mutually exclusive.

---

[33] Hence UML doesn't have an IOR merge element, unlike some other modeling languages.

7. SOME MORE BITS AND PIECES ON FLOW CONTROL

A few more interesting bits and pieces about modeling Business Processes with Actions and Activities. For those who want or need to know.

This chapter completes the coverage of control flow modeling of Business Processes using UML Activities.

7.1 Ad-hoc Business Processes

In the examples seen so far there is a very definite *workflow* character to the process being described. Workflow is the notion of a process where there is a strong sense of a sequence being followed, albeit there may be different sequence paths to follow.

The vast majority of Business Processes are workflow in nature, but not all of them. And even processes that have overall workflow characteristics may have Sub-Processes and Tasks that have not. The diagram in Fig. 25 illustrates a Sub-Process that could be characterized as *ad-hoc*[34]; i.e. all the Sub-Process Tasks have to be done at some point, but many of them do not have to be done in any particular pre-defined order. Furthermore many of the Tasks may be performed in parallel.

In Fig. 25, which is a fragment of a complete diagram, we imagine that once a holiday is booked, there are several steps involved in taking and enjoying the holiday. One of these is *'Prepare for Holiday'* which involves a number of Tasks, all of which must be done before the day of departure, but most of them do not need to be done in any particular order.

---

[34] The term 'ad-hoc' is commonly used to indicate a Business Process that is not workflow-like. This is not a UML term, however, I discovered it in BPMN.

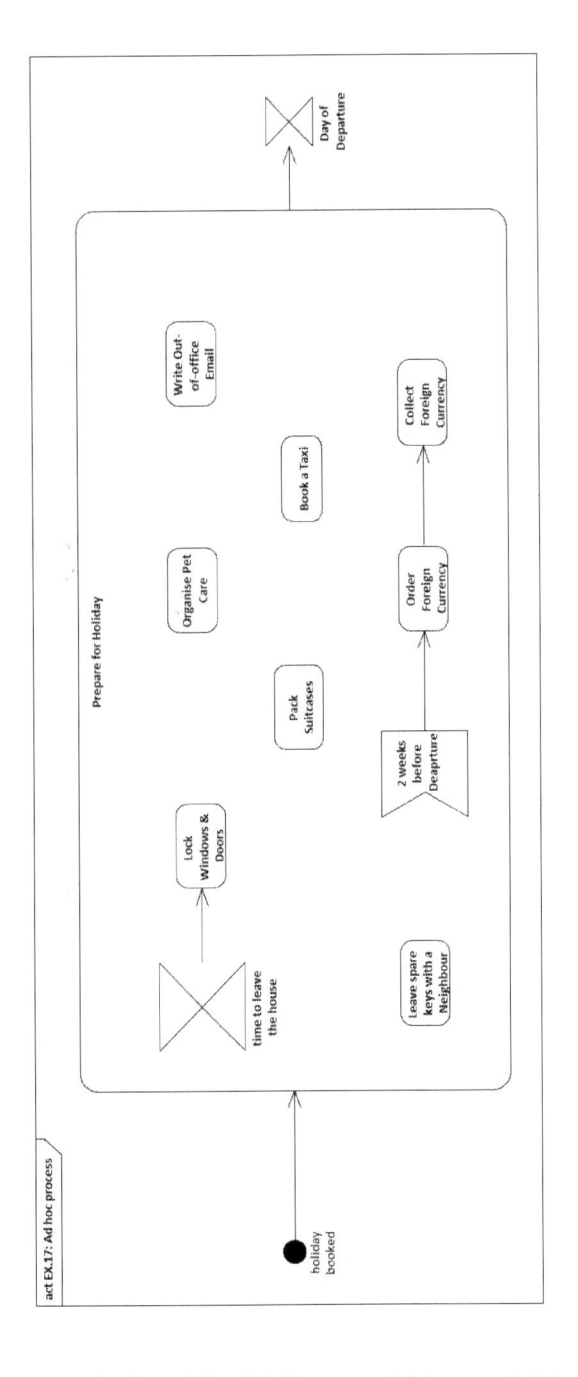

Figure 25: Example of an ad-hoc Sub-Process modeled as an Activity (fragment).

There are a couple of interesting things about the Sub-Process *'Prepare for Holiday'*, which is modelled as an Activity:

-When the Activity is instantiated, all the Actions *without* an in-bound control flow are activated immediately and each possesses a token. They execute in parallel; Actions in any Activity are intrinsically performed in parallel unless constrained by a control flow to be part of a sequence:

> *"When an Activity is first invoked, none of its nodes other than input ActivityParameterNodes will initially hold any tokens. However, nodes that do not have incoming edges and require no input data to execute are immediately enabled. A single control token is placed on each enabled node and they begin executing concurrently. Such nodes include ExecutableNodes (see sub clause 15.5) with no incoming* ControlFlows *and no mandatory input data and InitialNodes (see sub clause 15.3)." [UML; §5.2.3.6]*

-When the Actions without an outbound flow are finished their tokens cannot go anywhere. When all the Actions are in that state, the Activity instance will finish, and all the tokens will be lost. We might think of this as there being an implicit FlowFinalNode, wherever there is an Action with no outbound flow:

> *"The execution of an Activity with no streaming Parameters completes when it has no nodes executing and no nodes enabled for execution, or when it is explicitly terminated using an ActivityFinalNode." [UML: §15.2.3.6].*

7.2 Preconditions and Postconditions

Both Activities and their Actions can have Preconditions and Postconditions specified, which might be shown on the diagram as text. These are examples of the use of *constraints* in UML. Any element in UML can have constraints attached.

Preconditions described relevant facts in the environment of the Action that must be true for the Action to begin. Because they are Preconditions, the Action's behavior can assume that such facts are true, so the modeler may wish to inform the target audience about these assumptions.

Preconditions can affect token flow, in that tokens cannot move from source to target, unless the target's specified preconditions (if any) are *true*.

Postconditions describe interesting facts about the state of the system that will be true when the Action finishes. Postconditions could vary therefore according to how the Action ended. Tokens will only be offered on the output side of an Action, if the Postconditions are *true*.

Pre and post conditions may be 'local', which means they apply only to the instance of the Action or Activity where they are specified. So for example the same Action invoked in different parts of an Activity could have differing pre and post conditions. They could also be 'global', and apply to all instances.

These specification devices are useful for software modeling, but in the context of Business Process modeling, I advise using these features with care, and only specify them where they really contribute to the value of the model, and enhance comprehension by the audience. For example, it is very easy to end up with a long list of Preconditions in the context of Business Processes and their Tasks. Only list things that may not be obvious to the audience. I rarely find the need to use them.

7.3 Join Specs

A Join can have a *joinSpec* attached, formulated as a Boolean expression. This can appear on the diagram if required. If specified, the Join won't complete until all the required tokens have arrived on the inbound side **and** the Boolean expression which is the *joinSpec* evaluates to *true*.

7.4 Activity Property *isSingleInstance*

Each Activity instance is created with a Boolean property *isSingleInstance*[35]. By default this is *false* which means that every invocation of the Activity is a separate instance, with its own set of tokens. If *true* however, then, once instantiated, any further triggering events relevant to the Activity, will have an effect on the same invocation instance, resulting in the generation of additional tokens.

An example will make the effect of this property setting clearer. Let us imagine a Sales Order fulfilment scenario. The Activity to model the Business Process of taking and fulfilling a single Sales Order would benefit from setting *isSingleInstance* to *false*, so that every new Sales Order follows its own pathway, directed by its own set of tokens, which flow within its own instance. In such a case the progress of any particular Sales Order cannot be

---

[35] This property does not apply to Actions, but they do have a similar property *isLocallyReentrant*, which is discussed later.

affected by the progress of any other Sales Order.

But imagine modeling as an Activity the Sales Department of a business that deals with Sales Orders in general. Here it is more useful to set *isSingleInstance* to *true*, since, once created, the same Sales Department continues to exist, processing Sales Orders, until it is abolished. In this arrangement, every Sales Order that comes in will result in its *own* token being generated, adding to those already there. The effect of this is that its token(s) could possibly mingle and interfere with tokens from other Sales Orders not yet fulfilled. The Activity Diagrams for the two cases look quite different, as shown in Fig. 27.

isSingleInstance = *false* (which is the default) is therefore the correct option when modeling the behavior of a Business Process. *isSingleInstance* = *true* is correct when modeling the behavior of a Business Function or an Organization Unit. Note that in the latter case, all the Actions in the Activity would probably need to be set with the property *isLocallyReentrant* = *true* (*false* is the default) so that a distinct instance of each Action is invoked as soon as a token reaches it, even if there are one or more instances of that Action still running at that time. I will comment on the effect of that property later in the Handbook.

7.5 Activity Edge Weights and Token Traversal

Any Activity **Edge** (control flow or object flow) may have a *weight* specification. The weight indicates the minimum number of tokens that are required before a flow can occur across the **Edge**. The default is 1, if the weight is not specified. Until the minimum is reached the flow can't happen; when the minimum is reached all the tokens are transferred together instantaneously. The notation is shown in Fig. 26.

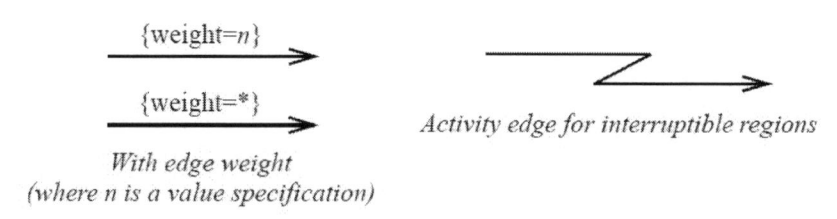

{weight=*n*}

{weight=*}

With edge weight
(where n is a value specification)

Activity edge for interruptible regions

Figure 26: Weight annotation on Edges [UML: Fig. 15.7]

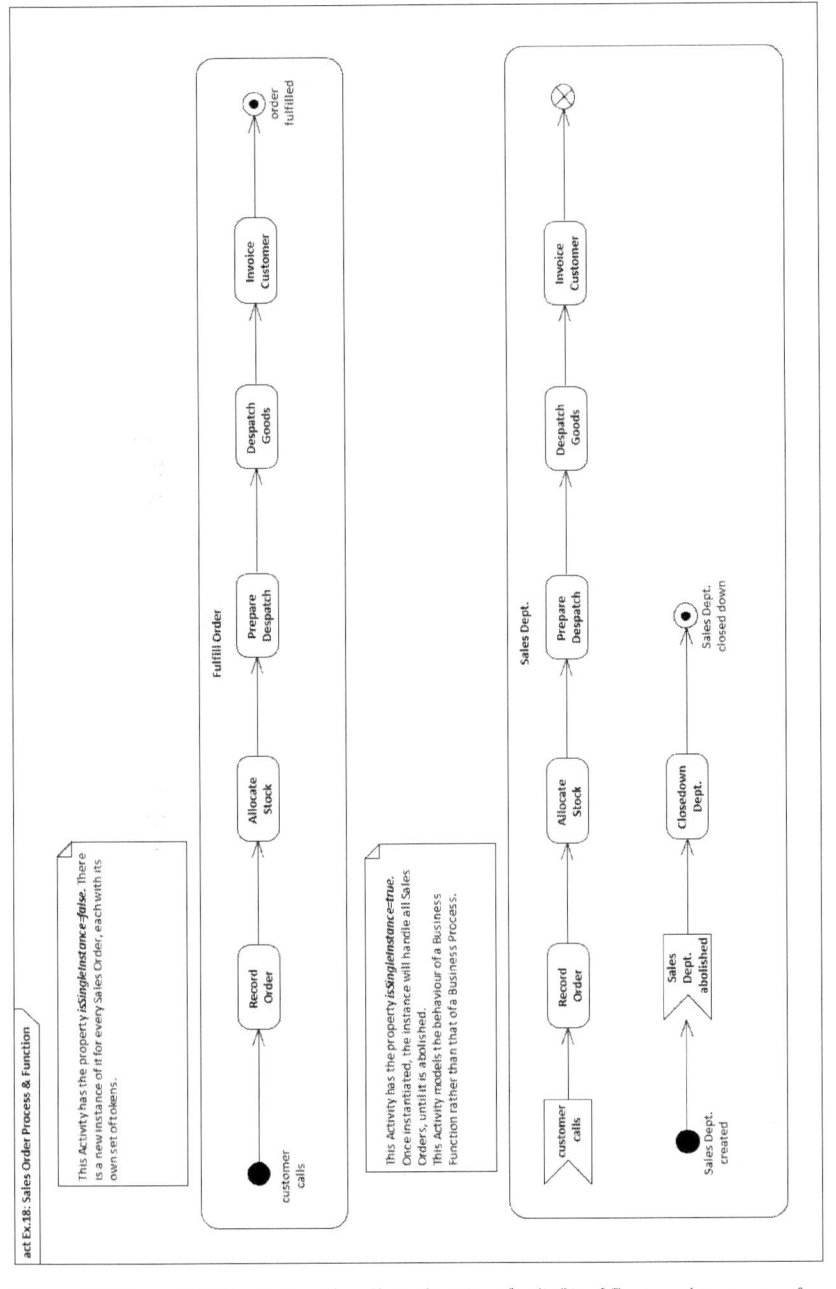

Figure 27: Example illustrating the effect of setting the 'isSingleInstance' property of Activities.

We can see an example of how this works in Fig. 28, based on the game of Cricket.

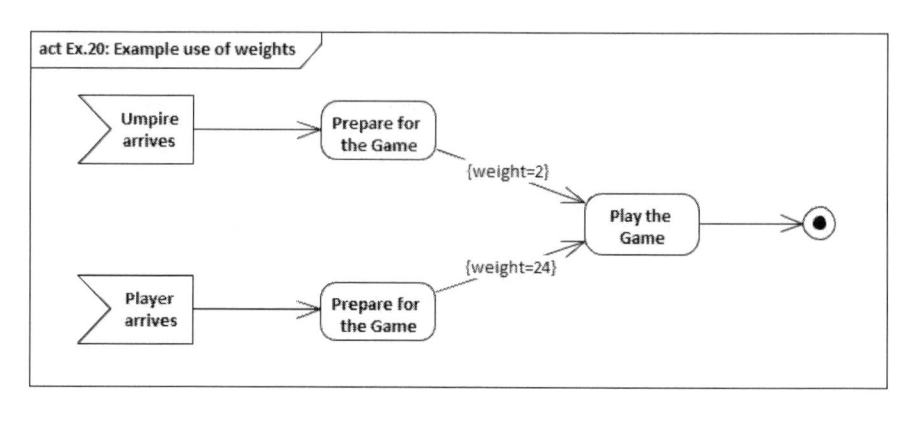

Figure 28: Example of using the 'weight' property of a control flow

In this example, once the Activity has been instantiated, based let's say on the decision to hold a game, both the **ReceiveSignals** shown are active. When an Umpire arrives, they prepare for the game. When a Player arrives they also prepare for the game[36]. However the game can only start when there are 2 Umpires prepared and 24 Players (2 teams) prepared.[37]

For this to work the 'prepare' Actions shown must have their *isLocallyReentrant* property set to *true*, so that each triggering of the signal invokes a distinct 'prepare' Action instance, within the same Activity instance. These Action instances run in parallel, each with their own control token. On the downstream side, these instances 'share' the same outbound control flow, and the applicable flow weight is calculated across all of them.

The reason we need this property set in this way, is because Actions cannot accumulate control tokens. If an Action's *isLocallyReentrant* property is set to *false*, only one instance of it can be active at any one time. In our example, this would mean that the first activation would happen just fine, but no more activations could happen after that, since the weight constraint would prevent that first control token from moving on. Bear in mind that an Action instance isn't extinguished (even though its behavior has finished) until its control token has moved downstream (or the containing Activity is

---

[36] Incidentally this example shows that Action names don't have to be unique across an Activity. This is because each Action is a distinct 'ownedElement' of its Activity.

[37] We will see in the next two chapters that the Activity of Fig. 28 could be modelled instead by using object nodes and flows, combining with control flows.

terminated).

These subtleties become clearer, once the logic of how tokens actually move along **Edges** is understood. The *source* of an Activity **Edge** offers the required number of tokens to its *target* via the connecting **Edge**. However, the target has to be ready to receive the tokens, and any constraints imposed on the **Edge** must hold true, before any transfer of tokens actually takes place. **Edges** themselves cannot hold or store tokens, and all the required tokens are moved together. These rules are governed by the *traversal-to-completion* principle in UML.

A weight of '*' (unlimited), means any number of tokens offered together by the source will be accepted by the target, all other things being equal.

7.6 Using Activity Diagrams to model Level 1 and Level 3 Behavior

So far I have concentrated on using Activity Diagrams to model Level 2 enterprise behaviors, which are Business Processes. This is the focus of the Handbook, but it's interesting to point the way to using UML Activities to model behavior at other levels.

The Task is the Business Process modelling device generally used at Level 3. It has the characteristic of being performed as an 'atomic' business transaction (**O**ne **P**erson, **O**ne **P**lace, **O**ne **T**ime). A Task generally breaks down into a sequence of steps or 'work instructions'. The logic of the sequence may be complex enough to warrant a supporting Activity Diagram, but equally non-UML techniques like Structured English, Pseudocode and Decision Tables can be, and often are, used (see *Opaque* Actions below). Another option to consider is the use of **StructuredActivityNodes**, which I will explain in a later chapter.

Level 3 is the level at which UML Use Cases could be defined as a way to specify IT software requirements. Use Case narratives may be supported by Activity Diagrams. If both Business Analysts and Systems Analysts are accustomed to creating and reading Activity Diagrams, that will surely facilitate communication in an area of software development famous for unfortunate misunderstandings!

Level 1 is associated with modeling the first tier of behaviors required by the enterprise for it to accomplish its Mission/Value Proposition. There are two key concepts that are usually modelled here:

-Value Streams (VS), made up of Value Stream Stages (VSS).
-Capabilities, which are the structures required to execute VS/VSS.

A Capability identifies what an enterprise needs to be able to do, in view of its Mission and strategy, and a VSS gives a label to the 'doing'. A VS is a linking of VSS to create value for stakeholder(s). Some VS serve the end Customer of the enterprise, others serve other stakeholders. Since each VSS requires a Capability to execute it, a VS could also be seen as a linking of Capabilities[38].

The diagram in Fig. 29 makes a very light use of Activity diagramming to represent a well-known Value Stream *'Hire to Retire'*, as an example. This VS maps out the Actions (which invoke Activities) performed on and for an employee (Team Member), from recruitment until retirement from a company. The collection of Actions shown deals with events that occur relating to a Team Member's employment with a company. This Activity should have the property *isSingleInstance* set to *true*, since once instantiated we imagine the VS continues to exist unless it is abolished.

Fig. 29 is a Level 1 diagram, so it does not show a 'flow of control', as a Level 2 diagram is generally meant to do. For example, once the Action *'Hire Team Member'* has occurred for an individual, it probably won't happen again. The Action *'Assess Team Member'*, by contrast, might occur every quarter for the rest of their employment. Clearly 'hire' has to happen before 'assess' can happen, so there is *some* kind of dependency, but every 'assess' is not preceded by a 'hire'.

The shorthand way of differentiating between models at Levels 1 and 2 is to have in mind that Level 2 Tasks have a 1:1 control flow relationship with each other in general terms, and the end of one Task triggers the next. Whereas Level 1 VSS have a 1:m, m:1 or m:n relationship with each other, based on data or some other resource dependency. The end of one VSS does not trigger another; some other event triggers each execution of a VSS, as the example shows.

To connect Level 1 modeling with Level 2, it's enough to appreciate that every Level 1 VSS will require a Level 2 Business Process specification to describe the logic of how that VSS is realized. Thus you can see in Fig. 29, that each Action is a *CallBehaviour*, and we would expect that each Activity called will have its *isSingleInstance* property set to *false*. You should be able to see how the Business Process example we have been following, *"Fill Vacancy"*, maps to the VSS *"Hire Team Member"*.

---

[38] I should not give the impression there is universal agreement on this way of modeling the enterprise. This is the field of Business Architecture, which is currently the subject of much discussion.

In terms of UML, what is also demonstrated in Fig. 29 is that every Activity is invoked by an Action within a system-of-interest. The top of the behavior hierarchy is the Action in UML, not the Activity, because only Actions are 'invokers' of behavior. This implies that at the very top of a behavior hierarchy depicting a system, there is, at least notionally, a single Action which is the system itself, seen as a single behavior. This model fits perfectly with a familiar notion of the nature of an enterprise, seen as simply inputs-transformation-outputs.[39]

Fig. 29 shows information «flow» between the Actions. This is a very coarse grained view of the information dependencies between the VSS. The flows also give the diagram that sense of it depicting a Value *Stream*. Another diagram of the same VS could show instead a more granular view, modeling the detailed use of **CentralBuffers** and **Datastores**, which are Object nodes used to pass data around an Activity. I will explain these and other Object nodes in the next chapter.

7.7 Action Types

In spite of their name, Actions are not really behaviors in themselves, they are **ExecutableNodes** where behavior can be executed or invoked. One could think of Actions therefore as placeholders in an Activity where a defined behavior can take place. Harking back to the terms I used in an earlier chapter, Actions are the fundamental form of Active Structure in an Activity.

UML seeks to maintain a separation between the behavior itself and the invoker of the behavior, so that the same behavior could be re-used by distinct invokers. This means that it is possible to define a behavior with independence from what or who will invoke that behavior, which is something we often like to do in enterprise modeling, as it produces more flexible and maintainable models. It also means we can use an Action as a placeholder in the Activity until we decide exactly what sort of behavior happens there.

---

[39] That said, every Action must have a behaviour context, so there is a chicken-and-egg situation here! The way I reconcile this is to imagine that the hierarchy continues beyond the enterprise.

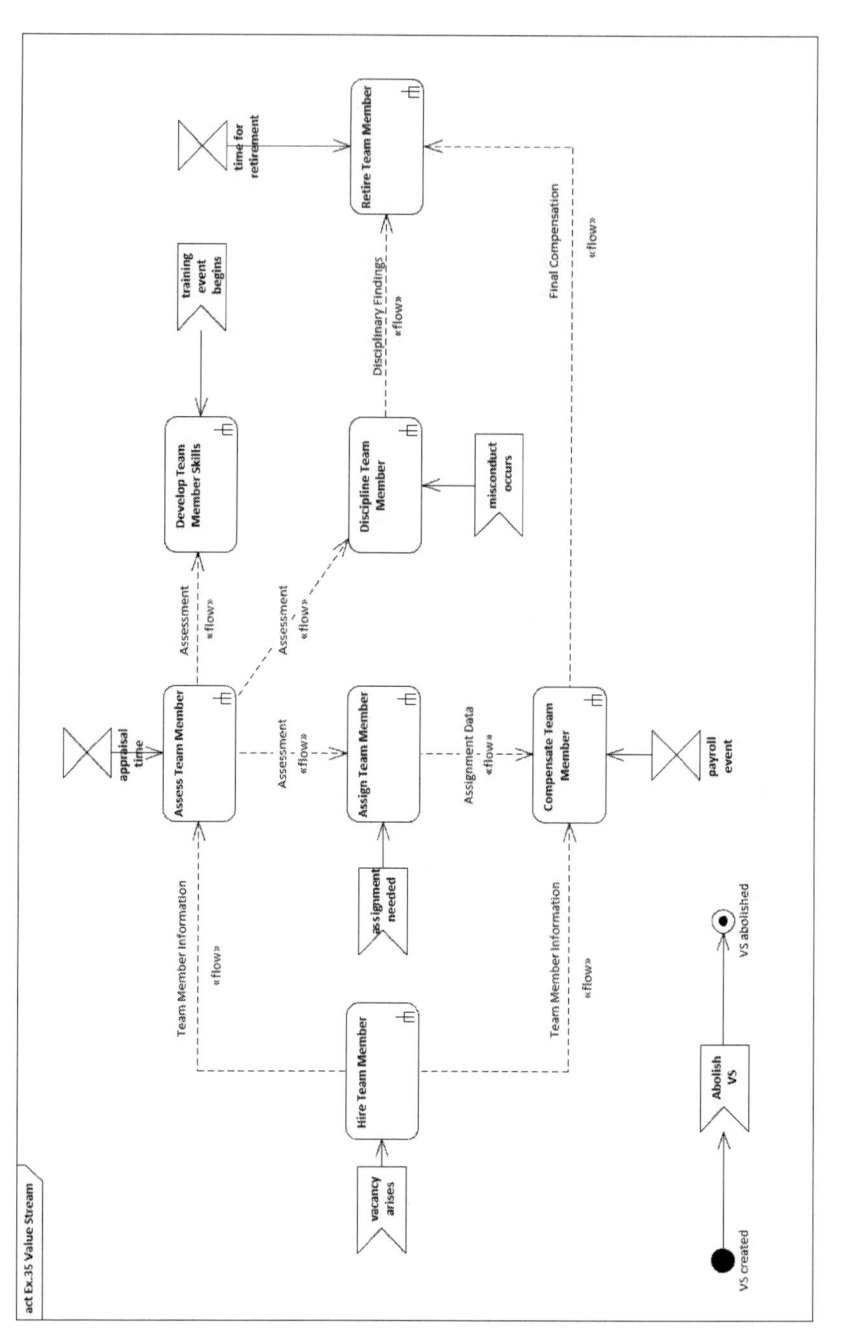

Figure 29: Value Stream 'Hire to Retire' as an Activity.

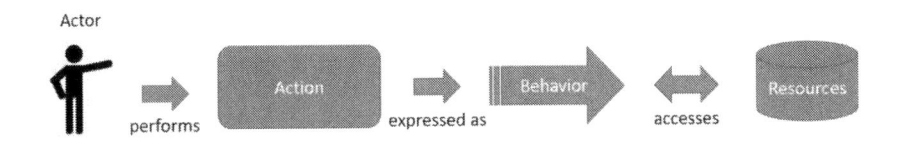

Actor   performs   Action   expressed as   Behavior   accesses   Resources

Figure 30: Action expressed as Behavior

This theme is illustrated in Fig. 30. If we assign a particular Actor to an Action (e.g. by using a **Partition**) we are modeling "this Actor performs this Action which is expressed as this behavior". This makes the model flexible and robust, since changes to the Actor or the behavior definitions need not interfere with each other.

When we insert an Action into an Activity, our tool should allow us to specify what 'kind' of Action it is. There is a long list of predefined possibilities given to us by UML, but in the main they are far too granular and software focused to be directly useful for Business Process modeling. This is a part of the Spec where the software bias of UML is quite evident. An Action has 'no kind' by default, it just represents some kind of behavior invocation. This is fine if we are sketching or even blueprinting, but all Actions would need a kind to be defined eventually, if we wished to generate software from the Model, at the implementer level.

Despite this evident software focus, however, those nice UML chaps do allow us to create 'user-defined' behaviors which gets around the issue of having to use these pre-defined software-focused Actions. Actually, up to now, I have been cheating a bit, because on the whole I have been blithely equating an Action, which is the fundamental behavior unit in UML, with a Task, which is the atomic unit of Business Process modeling. Apart from the use of Signals, this mapping is only really accurate if the type of Action is one of the following 4 kinds of user-defined behaviors:

  -The type of Action is an *Opaque* kind: *"An OpaqueAction is an Action whose specification may be given in a textual concrete syntax other than UML. An OpaqueAction may also be used as a temporary placeholder before some other kind of Action is chosen."* [*UML: §16.2.3.2*]. If a Task is represented by an Opaque Action, the steps in it can be described using Structured English, for example.
  -The type of Action is a *CallBehavior* kind of Action. We have seen this type already (the rake symbol). This kind of Action invokes a child Activity. As Business Process modelers we would probably want to reserve this type of Action for modeling Sub-Processes.

-For those of you who are object-orientated and/or service-orientated, a *CallOperation* kind of Action works too. The Action would call (i.e. invoke) an operation on an object defined by a class. The object could be an instance of the class which represents the behavior we are defining, or the object could be instantiated from a 'Role' or 'Actor' class, which are considered Active Structures[40]. The object could also be an internal or external service instance, with an interface, in which case we must know how to invoke the behavior, but we don't have to know the details of its realization.[41] A common example of such a thing is the use of a payment gateway.

-The Action is a StructuredActivityNode which I will deal with later in the Handbook.

It would be interesting to create a Profile extending Action types for Business Process modeling specifically, which would lead the way to defining 'standard' business Task types, similar to those defined in BPMN. As far as I know this work has yet to be done.

7.8 Initial Nodes with multiple Flows.

It would be reasonable to expect multiple outbound flows from an InitialNode to act like a Fork, but this is not the case, another 'gotcha'! Only one of these flows would get a control token, and which one is not defined.

We haven't seen an example in the Handbook of the need for this so far, but a modeler might want to specify multiple outbound flows from an InitialNode with mutually exclusive guard conditions, and this would work fine (remembering to have an *[else]* flow). This is the same logic, therefore, as using a DecisionControlNode right after the InitialNode. In such a case, the data for the test conditions must have been supplied via the parameters of the Activity, because there is no intervening Action to access or manipulate any data.

7.9 Using Signals for internal Communication

I have discussed using signals, SendSignal and ReceiveSignal, to communicate with entities external to the process. It is possible to use these signals to communicate internally too, although this is not at all common.

---

[40] The nearest thing to the term 'active structure' in the UML Spec is the concept of a 'behaviored classifier'

[41] Service-orientated architecture (SOA) has been mainstream in IT application architecture for quite a while. This style of architecture has many advantages in terms of flexibility and ease of modification, so these days we would tend to favour this style in Business Architecture too.

One example of the use of this is an *escalation* requirement. In this situation a lower level, child, Activity needs to escalate some information to its parent Activity, but continue with its execution.

The diagram in Fig. 32 shows a use of this modeling device, in which the Sub-Process 'Fulfil Order' deals with the preparation and shipping of an Order. This Activity is performed, say, by the Warehouse team. There is a shipping deadline Timer activated when the Sub-Process is activated. If the shipping deadline is reached, which would have to be before the goods are shipped, a signal is sent to a ReceiveSignal in the parent Activity. Let's imagine that when a CSR receives this signal, they inform the Customer about the delay and the deadline is reset. Because the deadline is reset, the need for the signal could occur many times (we have very forgiving Customers!).

Notice that the ReceiveSignal in the parent Activity needs to be active (i.e. possess a control token) upon activation of the Activity instance, in order to be able to receive any signal at the time the signal is sent.

Use this feature with care. A common error is to use signals to communicate internally across Partitions. As an example, let's imagine I fill in an expenses claim and email it to my boss for approval. The use of email here might tempt a modeler to represent this using signals, but this would be *incorrect*. Supposing myself and my boss are entities internal to the process, and modeled as Partitions, the correct model is just a sequence of actions, connected by control flows; *'fill in expense claim'* followed by *'approve claim'*.

Finally note that a sequence of SendSignal and ReceiveSignal connected by a control flow only works for external communications. It won't work for internal communications, because the ReceiveSignal is not active when the signal is sent. Verify this in the diagram of Fig. 31.

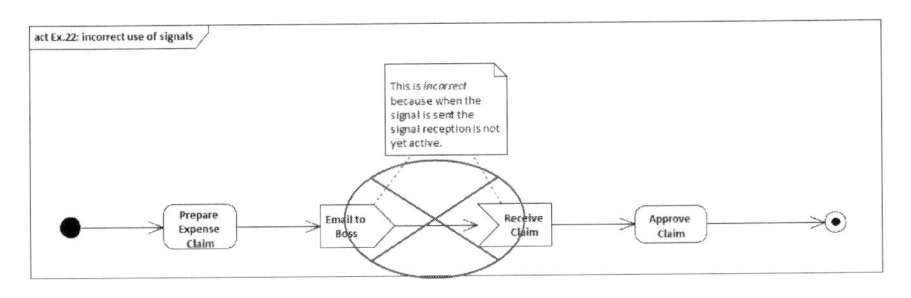

Figure 31: Example of an incorrect use of internal Signals.

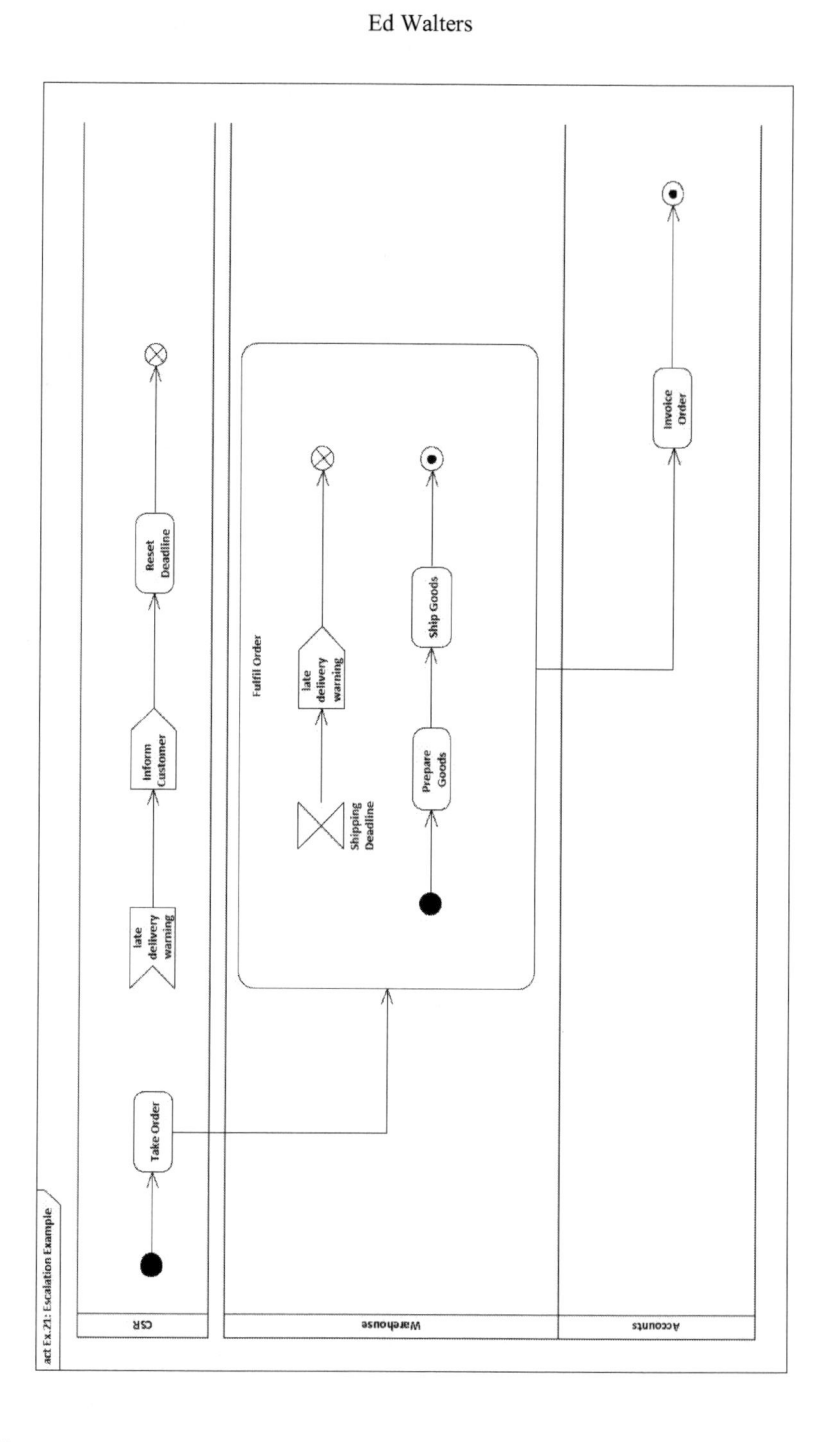

Figure 32: Internal Signal usage example

8. OBJECT NODES AND FLOWS

Brief overview of Activity features which model data flowing through an Activity. These same features can also be used to show the flow and manipulation of other passive resources across an Activity, such as physical items.

So far in the Handbook I have concentrated on the flow of control across the Activity from beginning to end. It is also possible to show data flow and manipulation across an Activity. Whilst both types of flow can be shown in a single diagram, it generally makes the diagram very cluttered. It is more usual to configure these flows as distinct Views targeting different audiences with differing concerns. Note, however, that the same Actions will be present in both Views of the Activity, because only Actions can manipulate data.

In these two chapters on object flows, I generally concentrate on, and refer to, the description of data flows, but you can take it for granted that anything mentioned that is valid for data flows could equally be applied to any other type of passive resource. For example, the flow and manipulation of physical items could be shown, to trace out the transformation of materials moving through a manufacturing process.

Data flow modeling might have the following uses, amongst others:

-Support for requirements engineering for IT application development.
-Support for the needs of Data Management, for topics like the data Chain of Custody.
-Support for the needs of Data Governance, for example the ownership of data, and compliance issues.

If you look at the Spec, you will see that a substantial part of the sections on Activities and Actions covers the data flow topic, so there is a lot of detailed stuff in there. In this chapter and the next I will try to summarize what I think are the most important features, and above all I will try to focus on the features that have some business modeling significance, rather than being software related.

8.1 ObjectNodes, ObjectTokens and ObjectFlows

For an Action node to activate it must receive at least one control token, as we have seen in previous chapters. However any behavior that is part of a Business Process will always manipulate data in some way. Indeed Tasks, for example, can fail if they don't have access to the required information. There is a famous acronym, 'CRUD', which describes the potential range of data manipulation by Actions: **C**reate, **R**ead, **U**pdate, **D**elete. ObjectNodes and ObjectFlows help to describe this manipulation.

ObjectNodes are a type of Activity node where data is storable in the form of ObjectTokens. ObjectTokens are like mobile containers that each hold a data value or a reference to a data object. The form and type of this data is very flexible, for example it could be:

- a constant value, like the number '3'.
- a global variable, like dateTime.
- an object reference, like Customer[42], so that an Action could read a Customer's credit limit for example.
- null, which is handy for those cases where the token might or might not have a data value; i.e. having a value is optional, and depends on the conditions prevailing in a particular Activity instance.

ObjectNodes usually have a type, which restricts the data referenced by the tokens it holds to be of that type. For example if an ObjectNode has a type 'Customer', it can't hold tokens referencing the number '3'. A null value, however, is compatible with any type.

ObjectTokens are passed around an Activity in a way that is similar to ControlTokens[43], but instead of flowing along ControlFlows, they flow along ObjectFlows. Whereas ControlFlows deal with the activation of Actions, ObjectFlows deal with the input and output of data to and from the Actions in the Activity. *Parameter* is the generic term used to describe the mechanism which provides input into, and output from, an Activity or an Action.

All ObjectNodes can hold multiple ObjectTokens and have properties that can be set concerning the minimum and maximum number of tokens that can be held (default 1 in both cases), and the ordering of the tokens in the node, such as FIFO (the default) and LIFO.

There are 4 types of ObjectNode: Pins, CentralBuffers, DataStores and ActivityParameterNodes. Let's review these types and their uses.

8.2 Pins

A Pin represents an input into an Action or an output from an Action.

---

[42] For the purposes of this part of the Handbook an *object* is a collection of data attributes. So for example a Customer object is represented in an object token as a reference that points to a group of attributes held somewhere, that describe the properties of any Customer.

[43] Similar, but not identical. There are one or two 'gotchas' here to trap the unwary!

"An InputPin represents an input, while an OutputPin represents an output." [UML: §16.2.3.3].

Also:

"A Pin is a kind of ObjectNode (see sub clause 15.4), so it holds object tokens that contain values of a specified Type (see sub clause 15.2 about tokens)."[UML: §16.2.3.3].

A Pin is owned by an Action, and represents the input or output parameters to the Action – InputPin and OutputPin respectively.

An Action can have multiple Pins. This would have to be the case if there were multiple parameters of different types as inputs or outputs.

There are 2 notations used for Pins, which are shown in Fig. 33 and 34.

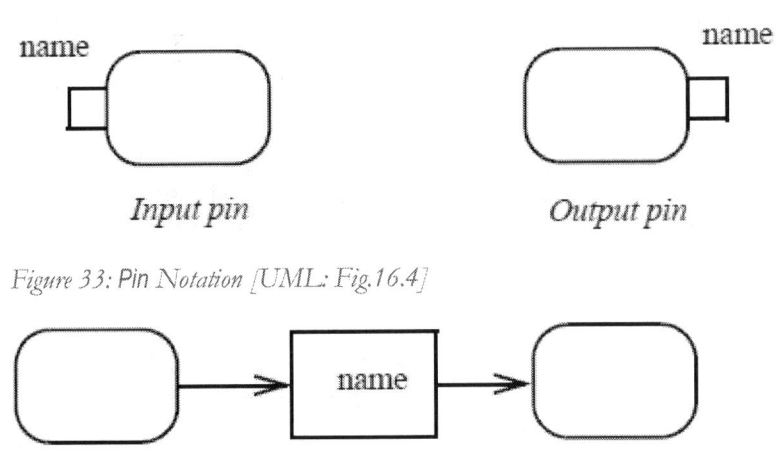

Figure 33: Pin Notation [UML: Fig.16.4]

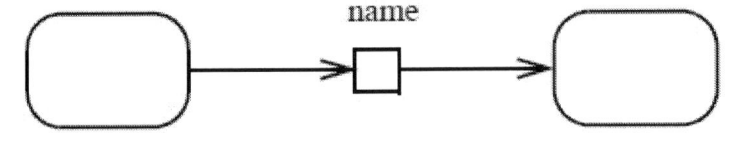

Figure 34: "Standalone" Pin Notation [UML: Fig.16.6]

The second style of notation, Fig. 34, is useful as a shorthand form when the output of one Action is identical to the input of another Action, which is a common occurrence in Activities.

The diagram in Fig. 35 shows a simple example of the use of Pins for data flow modeling, adding them to an Activity example from an earlier chapter (cf. Fig. 7).

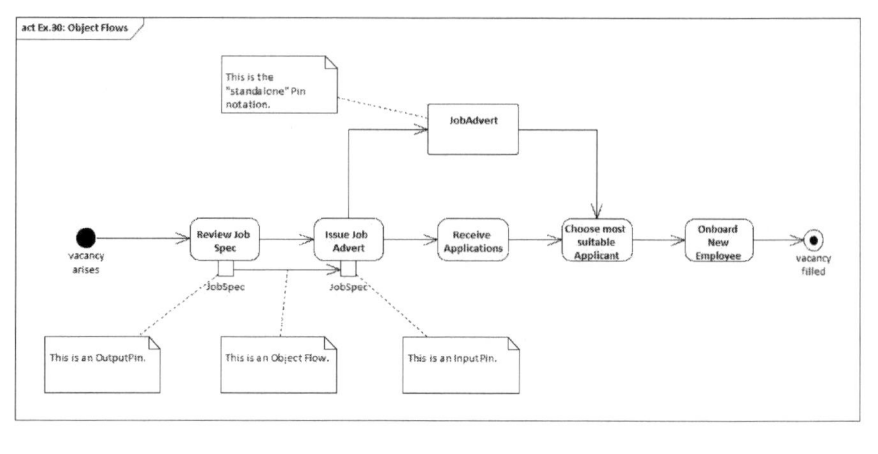

Figure 35: Example of using Pins in Activities

Notice that all ObjectNodes, including Pins, are rectangles, which distinguishes them from Actions which have rounded corners. This difference also makes it clear which flows are ObjectFlows and which are ControlFlows[44].

It's worth noting in this example, that the Action *'Choose most suitable Applicant'* will not begin execution until *both* the ObjectToken *and* the ControlToken (from the ControlFlow) arrive. Hence the AND rule for Edges on the input side of an Action apply, irrespective of what type of Edges they are.

8.3 Central Buffers

CentralBuffers are ObjectNodes which can store ObjectTokens independently from any Action. So an Action's OutputPin could send an ObjectToken to a CentralBuffer instead of sending it directly to the InputPin of another Action.

"A CentralBufferNode acts as a buffer between incoming ObjectFlows and outgoing ObjectFlows" [UML: §15.4.3.3]

Fig. 36 is an example from the Spec.

---

[44] Not as clear as I would like personally. When both flows types are shown, a different type of arrow for ObjectFlows would make things visually a lot clearer. There is also a case, which I will get to later, where the object flow *is* a control flow! However, with a decent tool you should be able to designate different color defaults for each flow type, and that would help.

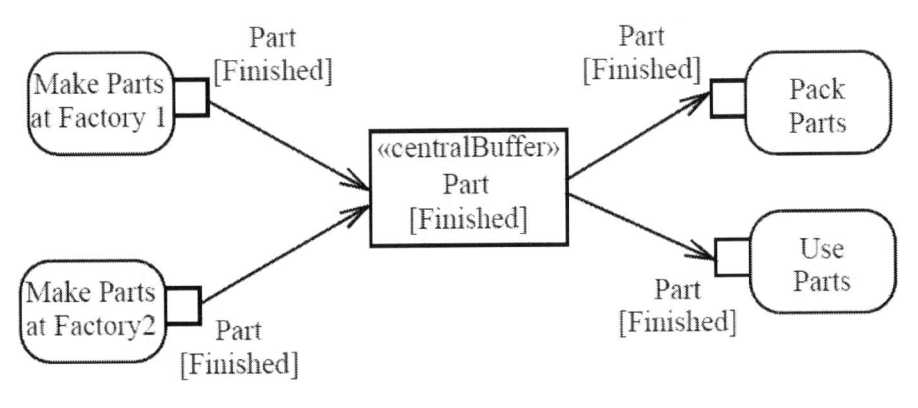

Figure 36: Example use of a CentralBuffer ObjectNode *[UML: Fig. 15.58]*

In this example, the CentralBuffer stores references to Finished Parts, in the form of ObjectTokens, received from similar Actions executed in two distinct factories. The CentralBuffer makes these tokens available to two different Actions on the output side. A 'Part' ObjectToken will only travel along an output Edge of the buffer when the target Action is ready for it (which could be immediately). The token is removed from the buffer when it travels across the Edge. Notice the use of the Pins in conjunction with the buffers.[45]

Notice the use of the *stereotype* notation « », which I referred to in an earlier chapter. What this notation tells us is that a CentralBuffer is a specialized type of ObjectNode. The state of the Object(s) in the ObjectNode may be shown in square brackets.

This example also shows one of the 'gotchas' in the logic of ObjectFlows. The flows to *'Pack Parts'* and *'Use Parts'* are not in a fork-style arrangement, as you might expect, so tokens in the buffer are *not* automatically copied onto each flow. What happens here is that the buffer offers tokens to each target Action. When the *'Pack Parts'* InputPin is ready for an ObjectToken, if one is currently offered (i.e. there is one in the buffer) it will be sent and removed from the buffer. The same thing will happen when *'Use Parts'* is ready to receive tokens. So these Actions are actually competing for the available tokens from the buffer.

---

[45] Incidentally, this example illustrates nicely how Activity Diagrams can be used to model the flow of physical objects as well as pure information objects.

8.4 Data Stores

A DataStore ObjectNode is a type of CentralBuffer in which the Object tokens *are* copied onto the outbound flows when the target Action can accept them, and therefore they are not removed from the store. This permits, for example, the modeling of data which needs be made available in a specific state to multiple Actions in the same Activity .

Another important difference between DataStores and CentralBuffers is that an ObjectToken arriving at a store holding the same data value or reference as a token already in the store, will overwrite the token in the store. So for example if there was a token pointing to a particular Order object already held in the store, and another token arrived pointing to the same Order object, then the new token would replace the old one. By contrast in a CentralBuffer both tokens would be stored, so modelers must be alert to this.

It is important to realize that DataStores do *not* represent persistent data directly[46], which many people might assume from the name. Only Actions are able to perform CRUD[47] operations on persistent data. Actions load/unload persistent data into and out of all ObjectNodes, according to the Action type. Bear in mind that all tokens are lost at the end of an Activity instance, and that goes for Object tokens as well as for Control tokens. An Object token holds a value or *points to* some item of data. So for example, if an Object token's data value was changed by an Activity's Actions, but that new value was not persisted by some Action explicitly, then the effect is lost when the Activity instance is destroyed.

In Fig. 37 there is an example using DataStores, modifying the diagram of Fig. 35.

---

[46] Persistent data is the term given to data held in some form of permanent data storage. So once created, it persists, until it is modified or removed.
[47] Create, Read, Update, Delete. In fact these four are collectively called 'effects' in an Activity, and could appear on the diagram, especially alongside Pins.

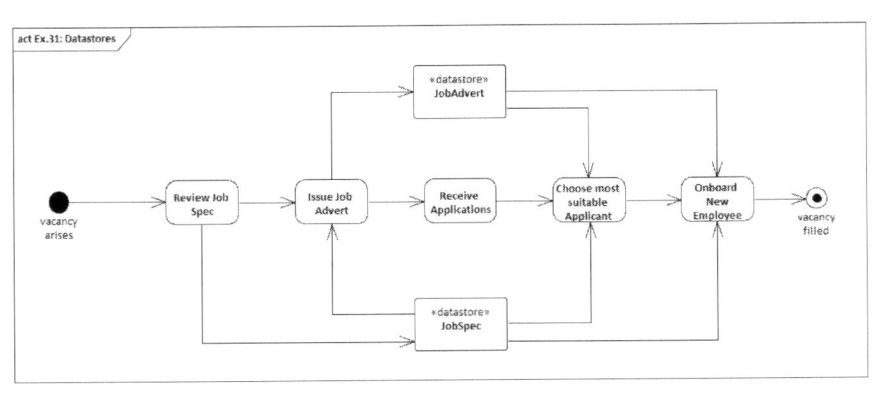

Figure 37: Example use of DataStores

Note that Pins won't do as buffers or data stores, because Pins are either input or output, not both. Also, as opposed to DataStores, ObjectTokens held in Pins are consumed by the Action they are owned by, once their execution starts.

Also note that DataStores (and for that matter CentralBuffers) are only ever read or updated at the start or end of an Action, and therefore never during its execution.[48]

8.5 Activity Parameter Nodes

Activity parameters are values passed into and out of an Activity. Parameters may be *in*, *out* or *inout*. When the Activity is invoked, values for the *in* and *inout* parameters are passed in. When the Activity execution finishes, values are returned to the invoker via the *out*, or *inout* parameters. This is one way, for example, a parent Activity can communicate data values to a child Activity and vice versa.

Parameters are represented using ObjectNodes called ActivityParameterNodes. There must be one such node for each parameter.

Remember that every Activity is invoked by an Action. The Action's InputPin(s)' ObjectTokens are copied into the corresponding *in* or *inout* ActivityParameterNode(s), and the Action's OutputPin(s) will receive a copy of any results of the Activity invocation, which have been placed on *out* or *inout* ActivityParameterNode(s). See an example of using parameters in Fig. 38.

---

[48] This is true even if the Action is a *CallBehaviour* or *CallOperation* type, because tokens are always local to an Activity. Tokens can't cross Activity boundaries. There could be several ways around this restriction of course, but I won't go into them here. Note however that StructuredActivityNodes, which I will look into later, are Action types exempt from this rule.

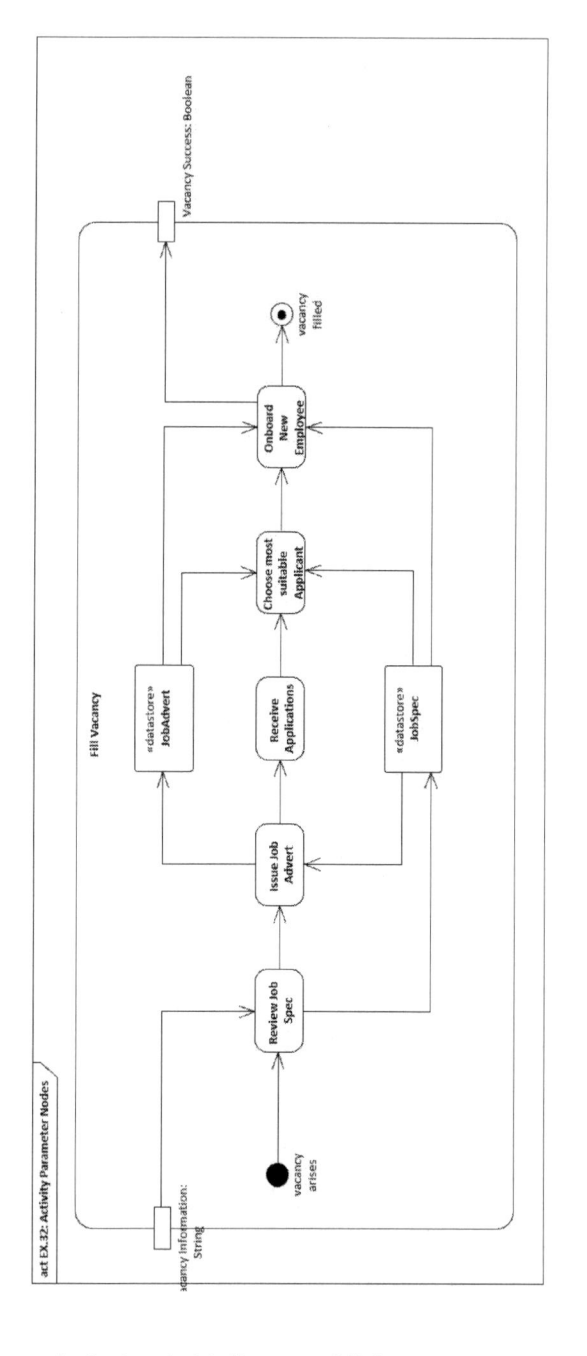

Figure 38: Example of using ActivityParametersNodes

9. MORE ON OBJECT NODES AND FLOWS AND SOME FINAL TOPICS

More on Object Nodes and Object Flows. Plus some final topics to complete coverage of the UML specifications for Activities and Actions.

What follows are a few more notes on features of interest available to the Business Process modeler, relating to Object Nodes and Object Flows, and also the odd final topic.

9.1 Control Nodes for Object Flows

Despite their name, all the semantics of ControlNodes with ControlFlows that we saw in previous chapters (i.e. Decisions, Merges, Forks and Joins) apply equally to ObjectFlows.

In fact ControlNodes can handle any *mixture* of the two flow types, but the rules for this are not straightforward, so I suggest this should be avoided if at all possible!

9.2 Pin Property *isControlType*

Having ControlFlows and ObjectFlows on the same diagram can make it very cluttered, so UML allows Pins to be defined with *isControlType=true* (default is *false*). The effect of this is that ObjectTokens can flow along a ControlFlow connected to such an InputPin, and the semantics of the arrival of the ObjectToken is the same as if it was a ControlToken (e.g. it triggers the Action).

Similarly if an OutputPin is defined with *isControlType=true*, the effect of placing an ObjectToken onto its outgoing ControlFlow follows the same semantics as if it were a ControlToken. In this case the single token is both a Control token *and* an Object token simultaneously.

This property is defined in the attributes of the Pin, there is no difference in the visual notation. Unfortunately this can lead to a certain degree of ambiguity in the diagram (but not of course in the underlying Model).

Fig. 39 provides an example of this usage.

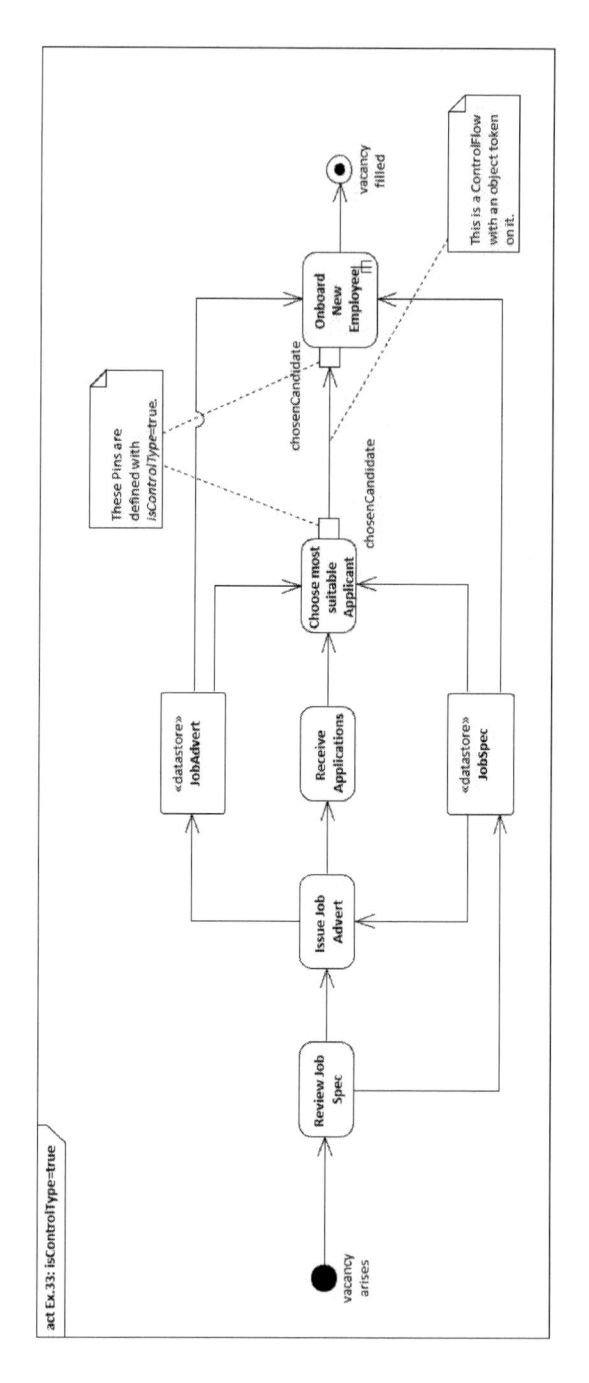

Figure 39: Example of Pins *with property isControlType=true*

9.3 Value Pins and Action Input Pins

"A ValuePin provides a value by evaluating a ValueSpecification (e.g., this may be used as a simple way to specify constant inputs to an Action.) When the Action is enabled by other means, the ValueSpecification of the ValuePin is evaluated, and the result is provided as an input to the Action when it begins execution" [UML: §16.2.3.3]

An InputPin designated as a ValuePin consults a ValueSpecification when the owning Action starts[49]. This means it won't receive any ObjectToken from an ObjectFlow.

ValueSpecifications in general are the UML way to execute a behavior with 'no side effects'. The idea is that they are simple query routines, so for example they could read in a constant value or perform a calculation or read the value of some Activity Variable etc.

In our recruitment Business Process example, the signal *'Send Regret Letters'* could have a ValuePin, which calculates the number of letters to send, and passes this value as an input into the Action.

An ActionInputPin performs an Action (which could therefore invoke an Activity), when the owning Action starts, so again that Pin will not receive an ObjectToken. Note that an ActionInputPin could therefore change the state of the system, whereas a ValuePin could not.

In our recruitment example, the Action *'Onboard New Employee'* could have an ActionInputPin to call an Activity that puts the employee on the payroll, returning an employee roll number that is then available for use in the Action.

There is no difference in notation for these Pins, but of course they are easily spotted, if they are visible, as they have no inbound ObjectFlows.

9.4 Actions with multiple Pins

If an Action has multiple Pins on its input and/or output side this normally implies an implicit AND. This means that ObjectTokens are expected on all defined InputPins, in accordance with the specified minimum multiplicity, before the Action execution can take place. ObjectTokens will be placed on all OutputPins, once the Action execution finishes. However, Pins defined as ValuePins or ActionInputPins are not taken into account in this logic (because they need the Action to begin before their logic is triggered).

---

[49] Note therefore that this type of Pin is not available for output, which seems rather strange.

Note therefore that for an Action to begin executing it must generally have received all its specified ControlTokens and ObjectTokens. However Pins can be organized into ParameterSets, which have the logic of OR. I will discuss this in a later section.

A rather subtle restriction is imposed on multiple InputPins owned by an Action within an Activity, in that all the Pins must accept their tokens simultaneously. For example if there were two InputPins owned by an Action, a token would not be allowed to arrive at one Pin and wait there for a token to arrive at the other Pin. This is in order to prevent deadlock situations where, let's say, two Actions are competing for the same tokens, and neither can start because each has a token that the other needs. [UML: §16.2.3.4].[50]

9.5 Variables

Another way of passing data around an Activity is by using Variables. This feature might be used on its own or complement the use of ObjectFlows. The modeler can define Variables for an Activity, and then its Actions can set, read and update the values stored in those Variables.[51]

Variables are local to the Activity, and therefore not visible beyond the scope of the Activity instance.[52] There is no standard UML notation for Variables.

Don't confuse Variables with the UML-defined Activity properties that are documented in the UML metamodel. Variables are modeler defined and specific to a particular Activity definition.

In our recruitment Business Process example, a Variable could be specified to hold the number of applications received. The ReceiveSignal *'application received'* could update this Variable every time it is triggered (for example via an ActionInputPin) and this value could then be read by subsequent ControlNodes and Actions.

9.6 Structured Activity Nodes

Earlier in the Handbook, I discussed various types of Action. You may recall that UML offers a number of pre-defined Action types as well as types that allow for modeler-defined behaviors.

---

[50] This deadlock pattern has a name: the *Dining Philosopher's Problem,* which goes something like this: imagine 2 diners sitting down to eat. A knife and a fork is required to eat, but there is only 1 knife and 1 fork. If one diner has the knife and the other has the fork, then neither can eat!
[51] There are specific Action types that do this.
[52] I assume this means a child Activity could access the Variables of the parent Activity, but not vice versa. The Spec is not explicit on this matter.

The StructuredActivityNode is yet another type of modeler-defined Action. This type is an Activity Group (like InterruptibleRegions and Partitions), and therefore can contain Activity Nodes directly, without the need, for example, to define a *CallBehavior*. The notation is shown in Fig. 40, which is similar to that used for InterruptibleRegions. In fact it is useful to think of a StructuredActivityNode as a region, which is confined within an Action.

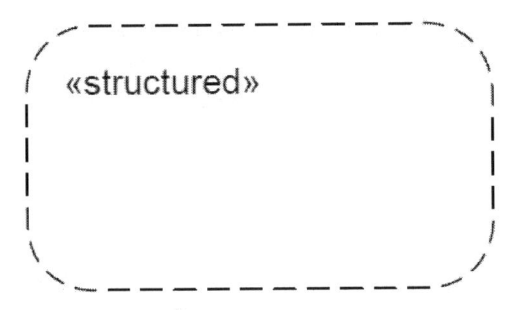

Figure 40: Notation for a Structured Activity Node [UML: Fig. 16.46]

Inside the Action node, Activity Nodes and Edges can be used in the same way as any Activity. However it is important to appreciate that this modeling is at the *same level* as the Activity which contains the StructuredActivityNode – i.e. this is an in-line expansion of the Action logic. One consequence of this is that Edges can flow into and out of this type of Action, if required, after execution has commenced.

There are, in addition to the general case, three specializations of StructuredActivityNode, which are sequence, conditional and loop node forms, these being the basic building blocks of computer programs[53]. There is no official notation for the specializations, but in practice, where these are made available in tools, we often see the Action icon split into compartments that deal with each part of the particular 'structured' form. My advice to business modelers is to avoid these specializations, as the semantics of them is rather intimidating, and they don't really add any value over and above Activity features that we already have.[54]

With respect to this Action type, it's worth recalling my advice earlier in the text on the use of levels to organize the complexity of Business Processes. Using *only* StructuredActivityNodes there is a danger that we will end up with everything being modelled at a single level. For sketching purposes

---

[53] Conrad Bock informs us that these forms were conceived for use by programmers, who furthermore were not accustomed to OO [7].
[54] This of course is just my own, very humble, opinion. Yet, I do find it rather strange that the Spec itself does not provide any examples of these forms.

however, this facility is undoubtedly useful, and one possible use of this feature would be to cover off the specification work required at the Task level of modelling, since this is the 'bottom' of the enterprise behavior hierarchy. The steps in a Task could be depicted visually by using a StructuredActivityNode, and you can see a simple example of this in Fig. 41.

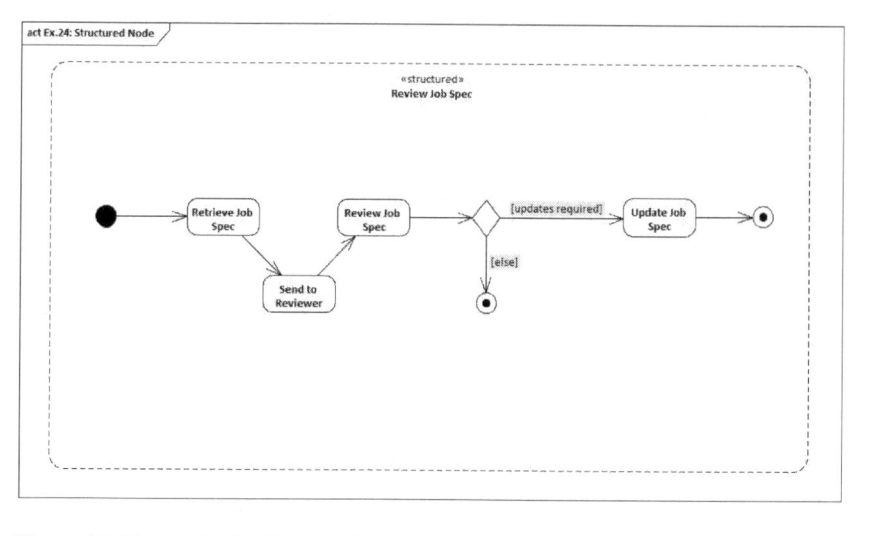

Figure 41: Example of a StructuredActivityNode to model a Task

There is one further specialized form of StructuredActivityNode called an ExpansionRegion which I believe does have considerable business modelling value, so I will deal with that next.

9.7 Expansion Regions and Expansion Nodes

An ExpansionRegion is a type of StructuredActivityNode, and is a very useful modeling facility where there is a need to deal with a *collection* of objects, which are represented by ExpansionNodes. It is one of the ways of showing iterative behavior in an Activity.

"An ExpansionRegion is a StructuredActivityNode that executes its contained elements multiple times corresponding to elements of an input collection." [UML: §16.12.1]

An ExpansionNode is an ObjectNode that represents a collection of Objects. The notation for this is a group of boxes, meant to indicate a list. Two common forms of notation for an ExpansionRegion with their ExpansionNodes. are shown in Fig. 42 and 43.

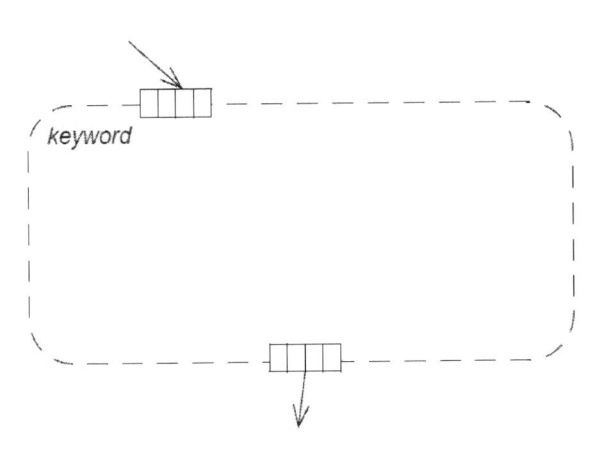

Figure 42: Expansion Region notation [UML: Fig. 16.48]

The form in Fig. 42 is used when we wish to specify the internal detail of the region. A shorthand form is also allowed, Fig. 43, where there is only a single Action in the **ExpansionRegion**. Hence this is a way to show an iterative Action directly within an Activity, if the iteration is over an input list.

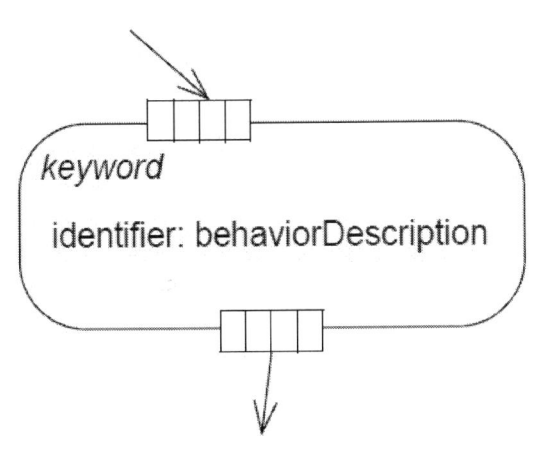

Figure 43: ExpansionRegion notation where there is only a single Action in the region. [UML: Fig. 16.49]

By way of example, let us complicate our recruitment scenario a little, to gain a sense of the usefulness of this feature for business modeling.

Instead of a single Action *'Choose most suitable Candidate'*, which we used on previous diagrams, let's imagine that we screen the list of applicants to make a quick assessment. Each applicant is marked for a 2nd review or is rejected. During the second review, we choose our successful candidate.

The diagram in Fig. 44 models these details, so let us deconstruct this and examine the regions in it.

In the diagram there are three **ExpansionRegions**: *'Conduct Initial Review'*, *'Decide Successful Candidate'*, and inside the latter *'Decide on successful Candidate'* which is a single iterative Action.

Let us imagine embedding these regions in the example of a recruitment Business Process shown in earlier chapters. Let us suppose that, once the deadline has passed for all applications to come in, the list of applicants is passed along a **ControlFlow** to the first region, as a single object token. The execution semantics of **ExpansionRegions** are the same as any other Action type, so as long as the (in this case invisible) **Pin** has *isControlType=true*, objects can flow along the **ControlFlow** directly.

The **ExpansionRegions** shown have the keyword *iterative* in the top left hand corner. *Parallel* and *Streaming* are other options. *Iterative* means that the Actions within the **ExpansionRegion** will be executed repeatedly, once for every item in the **ExpansionNode** list on the input side. The executions are performed sequentially. After every execution, the **ExpansionNode** on the output side will be updated, if there is an **ObjectFlow** to it. This then builds the output list from the **ExpansionRegion**. The input and output lists don't have to be the same size or the same list with the same objects[55].

Every internal execution of the region is independent of any other execution, but executions can share any common data, held for example in **DataStores** or **CentralBuffers** defined within the region, or even outside it. The key thing for the modeler to bear in mind is that from *outside* the region the set of Actions appears to be iterative, but from *inside* the region the modeling logic has to account for the treatment of any *individual* item from the input list.

A *parallel* type of **ExpansionRegion** will process all the elements of the list in parallel executions, rather than in a consecutive sequence (serially). However each execution is still isolated from any other, so the issue of token clashes does not arise.

Streaming is dealt with as a general topic in the next section.

---

[55] But all the objects in the same list must be the same type.

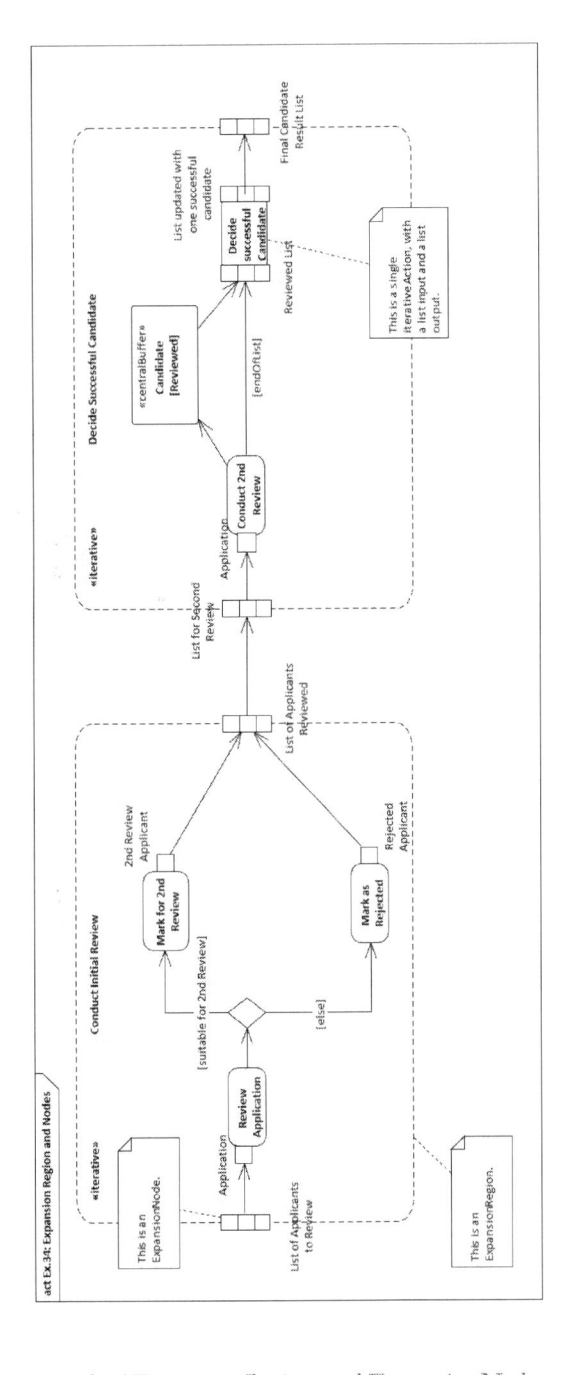

Figure 44: Example of Expansion Regions and Expansion Nodes

An **ExpansionRegion** is an Action, so having **ExpansionNodes** doesn't replace 'normal' Action **ObjectNodes** like **Pins** and it can use **ValuePins** to know things like the size of the input or output list, and similar collection-related data.

If an **ActivityFinaNode** is used within a region and it is reached by a **ControlToken**, the region's execution is interrupted immediately, and the output list is presented to the outbound **Edge(s)** outside the region 'as-is'. Be aware that this does not abort the containing Activity, it only terminates the Action instance.

9.8 Streaming

Streaming is the idea that **ObjectFlow** inputs to and outputs from an Action or an Activity can occur at any time during the execution of the behavior, and not just at the start and finish. In particular this affects **Pins** (Actions), **ActivityParameterNodes** (Activities) and **ExpansionNodes** (Actions).

Streaming defined on the input side of the affected behavior could produce extra object tokens, after behavior invocation, which would begin their course through the specified behavior, and mix with other tokens still active in there. On the output side, a streaming specification can produce objects tokens for onward flow while the affected behavior is still active.

Streaming parameters cannot be specified for any re-entrant Actions (*isLocallyReentrant=true*), because in those cases there could be several invocations active at once, so it wouldn't be possible to determine which one should process further input tokens. By the same argument, streaming for **ActivityParameterNodes** is only going to be useful where the Activity is defined with *isSingleExecution=true*.

The example of streaming in Fig. 45 is from the Spec. Note that *'Order Filling'* and *'Order Shipping'* are Business Functions, not Business Processes, and therefore these are Level 1 models. The need for streaming is likely at Level 1 whereas it is unlikely at Level2.

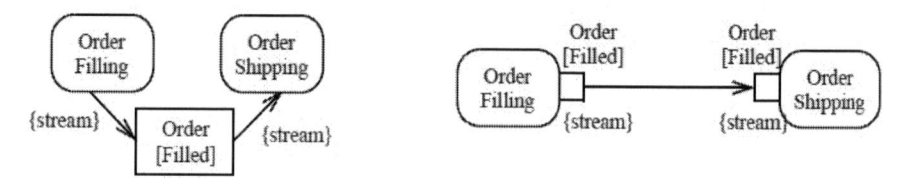

Figure 45: Streaming Pins example [UML: Fig. 16.26]

The notation in Fig. 46 is another way to show streaming **Pins**.

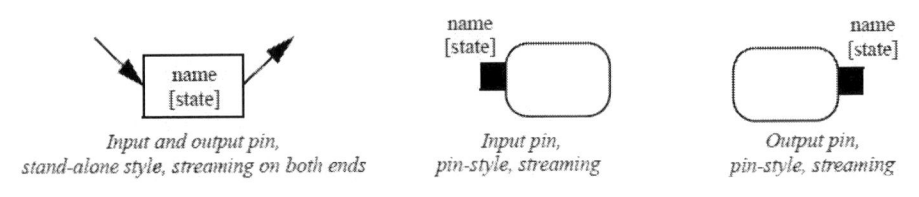

Input and output pin,   *Input pin,*   *Output pin,*
stand-alone style, streaming on both ends   *pin-style, streaming*   *pin-style, streaming*

Figure 46: Alternative notation for streaming Pins *[UML: Fig. 16.22]*

9.9 Parameter Sets

I mentioned earlier that multiple Pins owned by an Action have the logic of an intrinsic AND. This can be circumvented by using ParameterSets (Fig. 47)

Figure 47: Notation for ParameterSets *[UML: Fig. 16.23]*

The effect of ParameterSets is to create OR logic on the input or output sides of the Action. So it would be sufficient for ObjectTokens to arrive at the input Pins of one ParameterSet for the Action to begin execution (all other things being equal). Similarly only the Pins of one ParameterSet would receive the output from the Action.

Note though that tokens must arrive at all the Pins within a set, before the Action can begin. Note also that any Pin might be included in more than one parameter set, if necessary.

9.10 Exception flows, Exception Pins and Protected Nodes

An exception occurs in software when some error condition manifests itself. Exceptions interrupt the normal flow of things, and can be routed to an exception handler to be dealt with. This allows the software to 'fail gracefully', and produce a record of the causes of the error. Exceptions are (nearly always) fatal in software, so the affected software program has to be terminated.

Naturally therefore, UML has mechanisms for modeling exception handling of this kind. However, when modeling business behaviors, exceptions of the software variety, i.e. irrecoverable errors, are not the norm.

We saw an example in an earlier chapter of one form of 'exception handling' in UML, using an InterruptibleActivityRegion to handle recruitment cancellation. But cancellation is not really an 'error' in the same sense as a software 'error'. 'Exception' in this context is perhaps indicating something unusual or undesirable, but the process or Task doesn't 'fail' per se. We design quite normal business practices to handle these sorts of situation when they occur.

It is possible to define an 'exception Pin', as shown in Fig. 48.

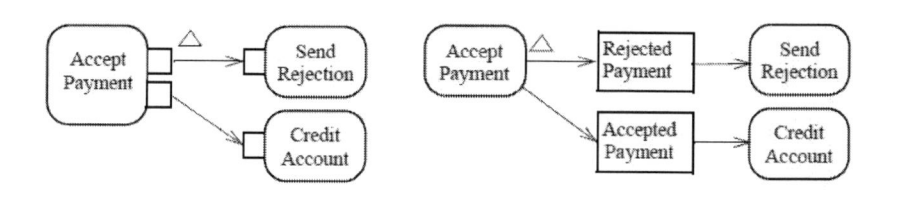

Figure 48: Example of the use of exception Pins [UML: Fig 16.27]

The 'triangle' symbols indicate exception Pins – but are these really exceptions? 'Exception' here means something more like 'the Action didn't reach its intended goal'. The Action didn't 'fail' in the same sense as a software failure. Note that as soon as the exception output Pin is populated, the Action itself terminates, and no data will be placed on any other output Pins (and therefore the AND Pin rule won't apply).

Another exception mechanism is provided by allowing any Action node to be designated as a 'protected node'. The notation is shown in Fig. 49.

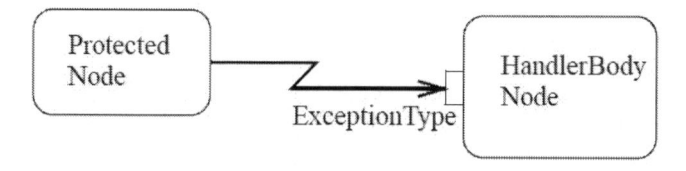

Figure 49: Protected Node [UML: Fig. 15.62]

Attaching the 'lightening' arrow, which we first saw used in InterruptibleActivityRegions, is sufficient to designate the node as 'protected'.

If the designated exception occurs within the protected node, the normal logic of the protected node is interrupted, and the node handling the exception, which is connected to the protected node by an exception flow, is invoked and takes appropriate action. When the handler node finishes execution, the control flow begins on the output side of the protected node.

At first sight this may look very software orientated, but one use for this facility in the context of Business Process modeling would be to enact a group of 'rollback' actions. These actions would 'undo' any actions completed in the protected node, if any one action in the protected node failed.

An example of the need to do this kind of rollback is presented by the *'Prepare for Holiday'* ad-hoc Activity, which we saw in an earlier chapter. If any of the Actions in that Activity fail for any reason, we might say "oh dear, we can't go on holiday!" That would mean 'undoing' any of the Actions that *had* completed. To represent this logic it would be sufficient to connect an exception flow from the boundary of the Action *'Prepare for Holiday'* in the parent diagram, to an exception handler node labelled something like *'Undo Completed Actions'*.

Note that the handler node cannot have any input flows (except to carry the exception object) or any output flows.

9.11 Object States

Any **ObjectNode** may be annotated with the *state* of the object(s) it contains. So for example a Sales Order object might have various states in its lifecycle that have business significance; 'open', 'approved', 'picked', 'dispatched' etc. If defined, these states appear in square brackets on the **ObjectNode** icon. This feature provides a link to State Machines, which are another form of UML behavior diagram.

9.12 Stereotypes «transformation» and «selection» attached to an Object Flow

Most of the time, in Business Process modeling, an **ObjectFlow** from one **Pin** to another requires exactly the same object. But occasionally that is not so, so an **ObjectFlow Edge** can perform a *token transformation* to pass on a different object to the receiving **Pin**. But note, this must be purely 'read' behavior, the **Edge** itself cannot change the state of the system (i.e. the behavior must have no 'side effects').

ObjectFlows can also specify selection criteria which control some characteristic of the way objects flow along it from the source to the target.

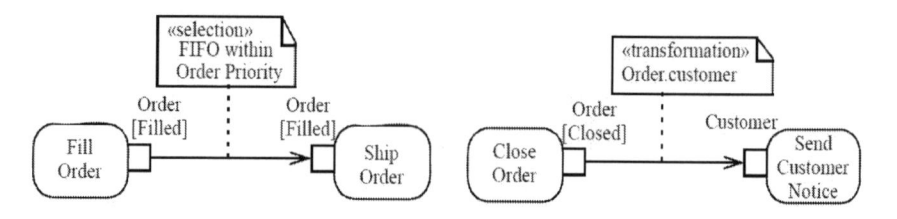

Figure 50: Notation for «selection» and «transformation» [UML: Fig. 15.16]

These stereotypes are part of the Standard Profile I referred to in an earlier chapter. Examples from the Spec are shown in Fig. 50.

9.13 «multicast» and «multireceive»

ObjectFlows have the Boolean properties *isMulticast* and *isMultiReceive*. The diagram in Fig. 51 is from the Spec, illustrating the use of these.

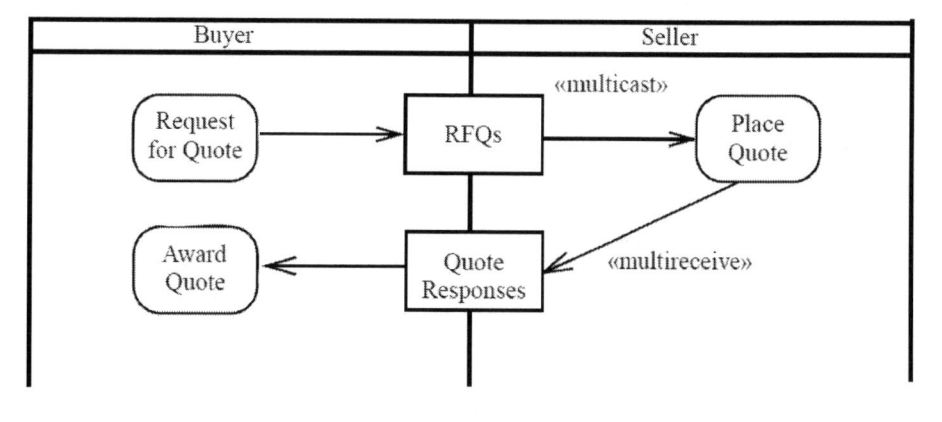

Figure 51: Example «mulitcast» and «multireceive» ObjectFlows [UML: 15.18]

The interpretation of «multicast» is that the ObjectFlow could be invoked multiple times; in this case to send RFQs to a number of Sellers. Similarly the ObjectFlow labelled «multireceive» could happen a number of times to model the responses from the Sellers. This then is yet another way to show iterative behavior in an Activity Diagram.

10. REFERENCES

Ref	Author	Title/ISBN/Publisher
UML		Unified Modeling Language. https://www.omg.org/Spec/UML/2.5.1/
1	Kernighan and Ritchie	The C Programming Language. 0-13-110362-8. Prentice Hall.
2	Martin Fowler	UML Distilled. 0-321-19368-7. Addison-Wesley.
3	OMG	Object Management Group. https://www.omg.org/
4	ISO 42010	ISO/IEC/IEEE 42010:2011 Systems and software engineering – Architecture description https://www.iso.org/standard/50508.html
5	Osterwalder et al	Business Model Generation. 978-0470-87641-1. Wiley.
6	Ambler	http://agilemodeling.com/artifacts/activityDiagram.htm

Ref	Author	Title/ISBN/Publisher
7	Conrad Bock	For example see: http://www.jot.fm/issues/issue_2003_07/column3.pdf
		Bock wrote a series of articles in the Journal of Object Technology (JOT) about the new form of Activities when they were first introduced in UML v2.0. This was around the time of finalization of UML 2.0, so some of these articles make reference to that process. You should bear in mind that some of the information in these articles has been superseded by modifications made between v2.0 and v2.5.
8	Arlow	UML 2 and the Unified Process. 978-0321321275. Addison-Wesley.
9	Eriksson – Penker	Business Modeling with UML. 978-0471295518. OMG Press.
10	Hammer, M	Beyond Reengineering. 978-0887308802. Harper Collins.
11	Box, G	Journal of the American Statistical Association.

11. ABOUT THE AUTHOR

 Ed Walters is a Consultant in Business Systems Development and specializes in modeling enterprises from many different perspectives.

Ed has a background in solution development and business analysis with experience gained principally in the manufacturing, transportation, and logistics industries. He holds a first degree in Management Studies from Leeds University and a Masters in Business Administration from the European University in Barcelona.

In recent years, Ed has become progressively involved with training, coaching, and mentoring clients in their use of Enterprise Architecture ideas, especially concerning how to specify and interpret Business Architectures and Data Architectures.

Ed's experience with using UML for practical modeling work goes back a long way, both as a software developer and as a business analyst. Ed regularly uses UML, along with other modeling languages, to model Business and Data Architectures, and helps his clients to do so as well.

Ed has expertise using ArchiMate, with regard to which he is an Open Group Certified Practitioner, and has written a number of whitepapers about the use of ArchiMate in different architecture scenarios. Ed is a Certified TOGAF Practitioner and an active member of Open Group forums.

Ed also has expertise in the use of BPMN, with regard to which he is an OMG Certified Expert in Business Process Management (OCEB).

Ed can be contacted via: truecom@ntlworld.com

12. TABLE OF FIGURES

Made in the USA
Columbia, SC
17 September 2021

45707610R00062